GET FOUND ONLINE

THE LOCAL BUSINESS OWNER'S GUIDE TO DIGITAL MARKETING

JACK JOSTES

Grow or Die Press | Boulder, Colorado

Printed in the United States of America

First Printing, 2018

Library of Congress Control Number: 2018906373

ISBN-13: 978-1-7321985-0-0

ISBN-10: 1-7321985-0-0

To Kara, my

TABLE OF CONTENTS

INTRODUCTION XIX

Sales Are the Lifeblood of Any Business...................... xxi

It's Easy to Be Taken Advantage of by Shady SEO
Companies. I Was. xxii

Know What You're Hiring People For xxviii

Small Businesses Get Big Results through Digital xxix

Take the Local Business Marketing Quiz! xxix

CHAPTER 1
HOW TODAY'S CONSUMERS FIND LOCAL BUSINESSES 1

Understanding the Local Business Customer Journey:
How Consumers Find Local Businesses 3

How Jane Finds the Best Chinese Restaurants 5

How Mobile Has Changed Everything Forever 7

CHAPTER 2
THE FOUNDATION OF DIGITAL MARKETING FOR
LOCAL BUSINESSES 10

Digital Marketing Foundational Elements 12

Branding 13

Website.. 13

Local SEO 14

Email Marketing 14

Social Media 14

Online Advertising 14

Other Foundational Elements 15

CHAPTER 3
LAY THE FOUNDATION FOR GROWTH WITH
STRONG BRANDING 18

What Do You Stand For? 19

Your Branding Will Be Seen Everywhere and
Influence Every Sale, for Better or Worse 21

All Sales Are Motivated by Avoidance of Pain 23

What Fears Do Consumers Have of Your Industry? 25

5 Branding Questions to Answer Before You Create
Marketing Materials 27

Crafting a Unique Selling Proposition to Attract the
Best Customers 28

Examples of Bad Branding in Local Business and
Wasted Real Estate 31

   McDonald's vs. Burger King 31

   The Kitchen and Bath Shop in Boulder 35

   The Refrigerator Delivery That Wasn't Very Cool 36

How ProMaster Handyman & Home Repair of Cincinnati
Won the Better Business Bureau Torch Award — Twice
.... 39

CHAPTER 4
DISQUALIFY BAD PROSPECTS WITH PROFESSIONAL
WEBSITE DESIGN 43

The Job of Your Website Is to Fuel Sales, Not Be a
Brochure 43

Contents

Your Website Must Be Able to Grow with
Your Business 45

Don't Shortchange Yourself with a Cheap
Website CMS 45

Things to Consider When Choosing Your Website
Content Management System (CMS) 46

    SEO 46

    Integration 46

    Site Speed 47

    Design and Other Customization 47

To Command Higher Prices, You Must
Look the Best 48

Design's Influence in Purchasing Decisions 49

How Professional Web Design Saved Jill Yellico's
Fledgling Business 49

Testimonial: The True Cost of Hiring an Amateur
Web Designer 50

Local Business Website Design Best Practices 52

    Make Your Website Header Immediately
    Helpful to Customers 52

    Use Clear Calls to Action to Help People Take
    the Next Step in Doing Business with You 54

    Make the Experience Exceptional on Mobile 55

    Have Your Blog Integrated with Your
    Main Domain 56

    Make Your Site Load Speed As Fast As
    Lightning 57

    Choose Quality Website Hosting 57

    Show Them the Experience Your Company
    Offers Through Great Photography 59

    Write Quality Content 61

Why I Love WordPress 61

How One Landscaper Uses His Website to
Stand Out from Chuck-In-A-Truck Competitors 63

CHAPTER 5
HOW TO GET FOUND BY YOUR PERFECT CUSTOMERS
WITH LOCAL SEO PART 1 65

Key Terms: Demystifying the Jargon.............................66

Search Ranking 69

Search Query...69

Keyword..69

The Anatomy of Local Search Results 70

Desktop Results..70

Paid Results: Google Adwords Advertisements.........71

Google Local Map Results: AKA 'Snack Pack' 71

Organic Website Results 72

The Golden Trifecta..72

Mobile Search Results from a Browser 72

Mobile Search Results from Siri 76

A Quick Rundown on Local Search Ranking Factors....77

Website On-page SEO 77

Local Directories, Apps, and NAP 78

Reviews 78

Behavioral Signals...79

Links 79

Claim and Optimize Your Google My Business
Listing...79

Think of Your Google My Business Listing like a
Mini Website 80

Contents

Five Tips for Optimizing Your Google My Business Listing..81

Google Confirms How Local Rankings Are Determined 86

Variety of Mobile Device Search Options Increasing 88

Customers Are Searching "Near Me," "Open Now," "Best," "Gluten-Free"..90

Get Found in Directories with Consistent Name, Address, Phone (NAP) Citations...91

   Common Issues with NAP Citations...........................92

How Tony P Lost 30% in Revenue from NAP Inconsistencies 94

How to Find NAP Inconsistencies.................................98

How to Attract Your Perfect Client with Keyword Research..98

The Criteria of a Profitable Local SEO Keyword 102

How to Become a Big Fish in a Small Pond................107

How One Webpage Created Over $200,000 for a Pilates Studio...110

CHAPTER 6
HOW TO GET FOUND BY YOUR PERFECT CUSTOMERS
WITH LOCAL SEO PART 2 114

Get Found in Search Results with On-Page SEO.......115

Google Ranks Web Pages Not Websites....................115

Observations about Organic Website Results.............120

   Web Pages vs. Websites...120

   Review Schema...120

How to Develop Your On-Page SEO Strategy Page-by-Page...121

   A Page per Product or Service.................................121

A Page per Event..122

A Page per Dentist, Doctor, or Lawyer......................122

A Page per Location and/or Geographic
Service Area 122

Local On-Page SEO Essentials.....................................126

Page Title Tags...128

Meta Description..131

Keywords in URL..132

Use Keywords in H1, H2, and H3 Headings 134

Use Keyword Phrases Two to Three Times
per Page 135

Use Geographic Keywords for Cities, States,
and Regions Served 136

Lead Readers to the Next Step with Calls
to Action...137

Internal Links 138

Optimized Footer 139

Help Search Engines Understand Your
Business with Schema 141

Links: The Missing Link between Good Rankings
and Great Rankings...146

PageRank...147

Domain Authority: A Metric for Measuring the Quantity
and Quality of Links 147

Links Represent Trust 149

Five Link-Building Ideas for Local Businesses 149

1. Chamber of Commerce Directory...........................149

2. Industry-Specific Directories.................................150

3. Vendors, Partners, Etc. 151

4. Write a Testimonial...151

Contents

5. Get Creative 152

Additional SEO Resources 152

CHAPTER 7
ARE YOU THE BEST? BECOME THE CHOICE WITH
STRONG REVIEWS 154

Reviews Influence Search Engine Rankings 155

Reviews Influence Search Results for
"Best" Queries 156

Reviews Influence Purchase Decisions 158

Consumer Trust in Online Reviews on the Rise 159

Reviews from the Web 160

The Words Used in Reviews Affect Google
Rankings 162

My Famous Chicken Wings Experiment 162

How to Find Out Where to Get Reviews 165

Gain Competitive Advantage with Rating Schema 168

How to Respond to Negative Reviews without
Sounding like a Jerk 169

How to Get Reviews 175

Why Are My Yelp Reviews "Not Recommended?" 177

Yelp Filters Reviews — And It's Actually a
Good Thing 178

What to Do About It? Get Good Reviews
from Active Yelpers! 178

Automate Review Collection as Part of Your
Sales Process with GetFiveStars 179

CHAPTER 8
DRIVE REPEAT BUSINESS WITH EMAIL MARKETING 183

Three Reasons Why Email Works 185

How Flatirons Carpet and Hardwood Got 10 Jobs
within the First Hour of One Email Campaign..............187

Stand Out in Noisy Email Inboxes with
Professional Design..190

Five Commandments for Better Results from
Email Campaigns...192

Generating Results with Strong Offers.......................200

New Customer Welcome...200

Celebrate Birthdays and Anniversaries....................201

Collecting Email Addresses to Grow Your List...........203

Frequency: How Often Should You Send?.................205

What Day and Time Should You Send?......................206

Selecting the Right Email Marketing Software for
Your Business...207

Why You Need Email Marketing Software and
the Problem with Sending from Gmail......................208

The CAN-SPAM Act..208

Five Factors to Consider When Selecting Your
Email Marketing Software...210

CHAPTER 9
LEVERAGE SOCIAL MEDIA MARKETING TO
ENGAGE AND CONVERT...215

Share Your Business Experience Using
Social Media...216

Document, Don't Create...216

7 Social Media Post Ideas + Real Local
Business Examples..217

Use Hashtags That Customers in Your Geographic
Market Use...224

Be Careful and Research Each Hashtag.................227

Keep Content Fresh with a Blog.................................227

Contents

Site Freshness..227

Internal Linking 228

Ideas for Local Business Blog Posts 229

Answer FAQs on Your Website.................................229

Recap a Conference You Attended and Relay
the Takeaways to Your Customers 231

After the Sale Resources...232

Ideas for Post-Sale Content 233

Stop Lollygagging You Have to Pay to Play 233

Why Facebook Advertising is Currently the Greatest
Promotional Opportunity for Small Business..............235

Facebook's Data Centric Partners Know What
You Like...237

Facebook Custom Audiences 239

Effective Facebook Ad Types for Local Businesses....242

Carousel Ads 242

Facebook Video Ads 243

Lead Generation Ads..244

Using Facebook for Job Recruiting 244

Creating Direct Response Offers That Generate
Results 245

Funnel Them into Leads with Landing Pages
and Automation...246

CHAPTER 10
STAND OUT FROM YOUR COMPETITION WITH
THE POWER OF VIDEO 250

For Purchases Requiring a High Level of Trust
and Investment, Video Can Make All the Difference...251

People Remember Stories, Not Statistics 252

Leverage Video Testimonials to Make the Sale.......252

Interview People Who Fit Your Ideal Target
Markets 253

How to Recruit Top Employees with Video.................255

Where You Should Host Your Videos + How to
Embed Them on Your Website....................................256

How to Decide Where to Host Your Videos................258

5 DIY Smartphone Tips to Produce Quality Video
on a Budget...259

When to Hire a Professional Video Production Company
....264

Hire a Pro for Pieces You'll Use Every Day As
Part of Your Sales..264

Create Engaging Social Media Posts with Video 268

Facebook Live 268

Instagram Videos...270

Use Video in Email Marketing to Boost Opens
and Click-thru Rates 270

CHAPTER 11
MEASURE RESULTS..274

Local Business Digital Marketing Key Performance
Indicators (KPIs) 274

Examples of Local Business KPIs: 275

The Growing Challenge with Tracking Local SEO
Rankings 278

"How Did You Hear of Us?" 279

Measuring Marketing's Impact on Revenue 281

Use a Sales CRM like HubSpot................................282

Put Custom Fields in Your Point of Sale 283

Run Coupon/Offer Redemption Campaigns.............283

Contents

How to Track Marketing Sources in QuickBooks
Online (for Service Businesses) 283

How to Measure against Expenses and Consider
the PROFIT Generated from Lifetime Value
(LTV) per Customer 289

The Data Won't Be Perfect...290

CHAPTER 12
MAKE THE SALE..**293**

Dude, Answer Your Telephone......................................293

Respond to Leads within One Hour to Increase
Sales Conversion 7x...296

Leverage Templates, Scripts, and Automation Whenever
Possible to Save Time..296

Develop and Manage a Sales Process 297

Show up on Time..298

CHAPTER 13
BEYOND DIGITAL MARKETING:
BE EXCELLENT. BE LOCAL...**301**

How to Deliver Exceptional Customer Service
Experiences 302

Be Part of the Community...305

Host Your Own Events and Speak At Others..............308

CHAPTER 14
GET STARTED WITH DIGITAL MARKETING...........................**315**

Focus: Start by Building Your Foundation 316

Take the Do-It-Yourself (DIY) Approach......................317

Have an Employee Do Your Digital Marketing 318

Hire a Bunch of Freelancers 319

Beware of Dude-in-a-Van: The True Cost of Cheap
Digital Marketing Vendors..323

Work One-on-One with Me and My Team...................330

Core Values: Ramblin Jackson's Core Values.........332

Take the Local Business Digital Marketing Quiz......333

Take Action, Now...333

BIBLIOGRAPHY..335

INDEX 341

GRATITUDE 350

ABOUT THE AUTHOR 353

INTRODUCTION

"You are in the business of sales and marketing, whether you like it or not."

- Jack Jostes

If you're the owner or marketer of a local brick-and-mortar or service area business in the United States, this book is for you. By reading this book, you'll know what you need to do to delegate digital marketing to your staff, agency, marketing vendors, or to take it on yourself. You'll learn how to make better sales and marketing decisions to grow your business, avoid wasting money on advertising that doesn't work, and prevent being taken advantage of by the increasing number of shysters in the digital marketing industry.

As a fellow small business owner, I know how hard running a business can be. Thankfully, throughout my journey, I've discovered and read multiple business books that have made all the difference.

Some I found through Google searches, like the time I frantically Googled "How to run a profitable web design company" at 3:07 a.m. on a December Sunday and came across Mike McDerment's book *Breaking The Time Barrier*,[1] which gave me an idea that immediately improved profits at my agency.

Other books were recommended to me, like Michael Gerber's *E-Myth Revisited*,[2] which gave me an idea to *develop systems* for my company's core offerings to free up my time. There are countless others. But no matter how they found me, business books have shown up just when I needed them the most.

My business coach, Al Killeen, calls the process of reading your way through business problems as "bibliotherapy." Whenever I've come to him with a business challenge, he's had a book recommendation that has helped answer it. Reading is powerful, and I hope this book finds you at a time when you are focusing on one of the most critical aspects of growing your local business into a thriving enterprise: digital marketing.

You Are in the Business of Sales and Marketing, Whether You Like It or Not

You may be a chef who learned how to make the most delectable sauces from a famous French chef. You now own three restaurants in one of the United States' foodiest towns. You are not in the business of being a chef anymore. You are in the business of marketing your restaurants and making sales happen.

You may be a recent law school graduate. You are going into business as a solo-practitioner focusing on family law. That's great. But you are not in the business of being a lawyer. You are in the business of marketing yourself as a lawyer and making sales. *Then* you get to practice law.

You may be a brilliant dentist pioneering the way through the latest cosmetic dental procedures. But you are not just a dentist. You are in the business of selling and marketing your dental practice to get new patients.

Sales Are the Lifeblood of Any Business

"I'm not really a salesperson" or "I don't personally enjoy using social media, so I'm not going to do it for my business" are statements I hear a lot of unsuccessful or failed business people make.

Sales are the lifeblood of any business. Unless someone is buying your product or service, who cares how good you are at providing it? Who cares where you went to school, how smart you are, or how wonderful your business is if no one is buying? Sales happen as the result of someone selling a product or service to another person who discovered you through marketing.

This doesn't necessarily mean that you are personally the one making the sale or managing your marketing, but as the owner or person responsible for the sales and marketing success of your company, you must have an understanding of what your marketing people are doing for you and how it actually results in sales. **If you don't know how to measure what's happening in your digital marketing, you will be taken advantage of**.

It's Easy to Be Taken Advantage of by Shady SEO Companies. I Was.

Like many entrepreneurs, I got into the sales and marketing business mostly by accident — a result of being unemployable.

Believe it or not, I started out in business as a milkman. In 2008, one of my first jobs out of college was making door-to-door sales as a milkman for a dairy farm in Colorado. Wearing a neat milkman uniform, I drove a two-ton box truck to my routes with paper maps and looked for signs of milk drinkers: minivans in the driveways and toys in the yard.

Busy moms with at least two milk-drinking kids were my target customer. I had memorized a brilliant sales script that started with a big cheesy milkman grin, "Hi, I'm Jack, the milkman from the local dairy farm. Do you drink milk?"

If I was asked that question to a qualified lead, I continued the interaction by handing over a free half-gallon of milk in a glass bottle and asking, "Now, if we could save you the time of having to go to the store and your babies could have the freshest milk in Colorado delivered reliably to your doorstep at the same time each week, would that be helpful?"

If the person said yes, I used the assumptive close: "Great! Let's do this: Why don't you just sign up for milk delivery and try it out. I'll write up an order for you and delivery will start next Tuesday. You can try it out, and see how you like it.

"Mrs. Jones, you and your family are going to love how fresh this milk tastes and how much time it saves you from carrying heavy milk to and from the grocery store. And, if you change your mind after I leave today, just give me a call before Monday and we'll cancel. No hard feelings. Does that sound fair enough?"

Beautiful. I was making some serious cash, signing up five, six, seven, and, sometimes, eight or even nine new milk delivery customers per day.

But when winter came, people were less interested in opening the door in the cold to talk to a salesperson. Then, the 2008 economic market crashed, and more and more people were home during the day because they were unemployed and not looking to spend money on expensive milk delivery.

I became bored with the possible outcomes of the question, "Do you drink milk?" I could care less how the prospect answered when I asked if she drank milk. I also soon learned from a naturopath that the reason I had suffered from terrible allergies most of my life was because I am lactose intolerant. (Imagine that, a milkman unable to drink milk!)

That heralded the end of one chapter in my life but the beginning of another.

I was playing mandolin in a rock band at the time and had moved with my bandmates to Colorado to pursue music professionally. I soon realized that although playing in a band is a lot of fun, it's not necessarily a great way to make a living.

Because I had studied journalism in college, I thought I would try my hand working as a journalist with a local newspaper, the Rocky Mountain News. To my dismay, however, I learned that the paper had gone out of business (after 149 years!) and no other papers were hiring young journalists.

The sales manager from the dairy farm had moved on to start his own sales coaching business. He introduced me to a guy who was working for a multi-level marketing SEO company that supposedly helped local businesses get found online through its online directory and PPC marketing. He thought that it might be a good fit for me and introduced us.

After meeting for coffee, I decided to get involved with the company. I felt I could combine my passion for writing and talent in sales for a dream job helping people get found online. So, I paid more than $750 to join this company, which I'll call Local Shad-Link. (I have to admit, at the time I had never heard of multi-level marketing, pyramid schemes, or Ponzi schemes.)

I paid another $750 to join a networking group that met weekly. The members promised I would get a return on my investment if I stuck it out for a year and showed up every week. Through the networking, I was introduced to several business owners, three of whom quickly became clients. I thought I was helping them get found by new customers on Google with Local Shad-Link. But after a couple of months, their ads still were not showing up online, and they began asking me why. Also, I never got paid the sales commissions I was promised.

I quickly learned that the company I had bought into didn't actually exist. Its website was down and its Facebook page has not been updated in months. My "Regional Account Supervisor" was nowhere to be found and did not return any of my emails or calls.

I felt duped. I had been taken advantage of.
The product I sold did not work. Worse, I didn't really have much money saved up, and the people that I sold to were not getting what they thought they paid for.

I called each of my customers to tell them the bad news. The first one, a local print shop in Boulder, didn't want to hear about it. The owner didn't want to meet with me or have anything to do with me for that matter. This was not the first time he had lost money on marketers who over-promised and under-delivered.

The other two clients, a local IT company and my sales coach, agreed to let me work off what I had sold them in trade. I wrote copy for their websites, helped them with their social media strategy, and designed email newsletters for them.

Considering that I was already $750 bucks deep into a networking group and enjoying the freedom of self-employment, I started what would later become a digital marketing agency: Ramblin Jackson.

While my journalism degree wasn't very marketable, there were plenty of businesses that needed the social media skills I had developed in managing and marketing my band over the years. I learned how to sell at the dairy farm and decided to just go for it.

I learned from other business owners that my experience with the shady SEO company was not uncommon. Quite to the contrary: People were often taken advantage of by others selling internet marketing services that didn't actually work.

I was determined to figure out how it *really* worked and, at a networking group, met a guy who claimed to help businesses get found in what was then called Google Places. His name was Jeffrey Magner, and he soon became one of my all-time closest friends, business mentors, and the person who taught me nearly everything I know about search engine optimization. Jeffrey owned Trumpet Local Media, a local SEO company in Boulder that Ramblin Jackson later acquired in 2013.

While I had been taken advantage of by the multi-level marketing company, I'm glad it happened. It sent me on a quest to learn everything I could about how digital marketing for local businesses works. I learned firsthand to be confused by how internet marketing actually worked and to be taken advantage of by a fake SEO company — something thousands of business owners experience every year.

Since 2009, I have spent countless hours reading books, experimenting, attending conferences, taking online certifications with Google, HubSpot, and Constant Contact, and learning everything I can about search engine optimization and digital marketing. Through my agency, I have worked with more than 300 local businesses throughout the United States. Based on my experience, I can confidently say that I know what works and what doesn't — and the process we have developed over the years works!

Above all, in growing my company from just myself to a team of full-time staff, vendors, an office, and all the related expenses of doing business, I have learned firsthand that even as a marketing professional, I am also in the business of marketing and sales.

I hope that, after reading this book, you can avoid the costly and embarrassing mistake of being taken advantage of by shady SEO companies and shysters.

Know What You're Hiring People For

If you decide to delegate digital marketing to an agency, vendor, or an employee, it's important that you stay involved in measuring the quality of the work and in monitoring the actual results of your efforts.

Far too many business owners decide to delegate digital marketing because they're "not computer people," but in doing so end up wasting tens of thousands of dollars by not being involved in the creation of the marketing strategy or in measuring the outcome of the marketing activities. After reading this book, you will be more prepared to make better business decisions.

Small Businesses Get Big Results through Digital

My favorite part about the work I do is knowing that I am making a difference in the lives of my clients. Throughout this book, you'll read no bullshit, tried-and-true case studies and interviews with real business owners just like you. For some, the transformation in their business that came as a result of digital marketing has been the difference between going out of business and thriving.

Take the Local Business Marketing Quiz!

You don't need to finish this book to get started improving your digital marketing! Take our free quiz at **ramblinjackson.com/quiz/**

Key Takeaways From The Introduction

- You are in the business of sales and marketing, whether you like it or not.

- Sales are the lifeblood of any business.

- Even if you delegate digital marketing to an employee or agency, you must know what's being done.

- Digital marketing can make a big difference for small businesses.

1

HOW TODAY'S CONSUMERS FIND LOCAL BUSINESSES

"The trend has been mobile was winning.
It's now won."

- Eric Schmidt

Smartphones have forever changed the way people make purchasing decisions. From quickly texting a friend to get their opinion of a local business to reading reviews on a myriad of directories to finding whatever they want on Google — and potentially doing it all hands-free through a voice assistant — consumers are more empowered than ever to research and select the best fit for their needs, all within the confines of their mobile phone. How can a small business keep up with it all?

The main thing to remember is that everything online is increasingly connected and increasingly mobile. There is greater transparency about the quality of goods and services offered because consumers can share their opinions more easily than ever, typically via online reviews. This is a good thing. It levels the playing field and pressures businesses to up their game.

It is important to think of digital marketing and generating sales as the sum of many separate but related parts. For instance, who cares if you have a $50,000 website if after people find it, they search for your brand name online and see terrible reviews that dissuade them from doing business with you. Nice website, dude.

DISCOVERY	ONLINE RESEARCH	CONTACT BUSINESSES	SALE	POST-SALE FOLLOWUP
Referral	Visit Site	Phone Call		Surveys
Search	Read Reviews	Directions		Reviews
"Near Me" "In Boulder" "Brand Name"		Contact Form	$	Upsells
Sees Ad	Watch Videos	Online Registration		Repeat Business
Social Media	Consider Competitors	Chat		Generate Relationship
		SMS		

Understanding the Local Business Customer Journey: How Consumers Find Local Businesses

Whether someone first hears of your business through a referral or discovers you through a search engine, they are very likely to interact with your website and Google listing on their phone before entering your store or calling you to do business.

According to a Think With Google study of 2016:[1]

- 76% of people who search on their smartphones for something nearby visit a business within a day, and 28% of those searches for something nearby result in a purchase;

- 30% of all mobile searches have local intent.

In the spring of 2017, the Local Search Association published the "Digital Consumer Study"[2] — the results of a survey of over 8,000 consumers across the United States about how they find local businesses. The study found that search engines, websites, and social media respectively topped the list.

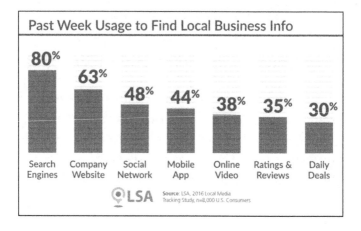

In July 2017, Google reported in their Micro-Moments series[3] that searches with "Best" in them have grown 80% in the last two years.

This trend of wanting the BEST result, with great speed and relevancy to whatever the consumer is researching, will only continue. Are you ready?

And no, it's not just those danged millennials glued to their iPhones searching on the internet for local businesses. Many people I talk with who have been in business since the print phonebook era find it hard to believe that *their* customers are actually looking online — thinking that it's mainly just younger people (who couldn't afford them).

I was invited in 2016 to present on the topic of how older adults use the internet at the Silver Business MicroSummit on a panel with the Boulder Economic Council, Colorado State demographer, and Boulder County Area Agency on Aging.

In my presentation, I shared research that adults in the 54- to 65-year-old range are the fastest growing segment of smartphone owners. I also shared the story of how we generated over $200,000 with one web page targeting seniors in Denver (which you can see later in this book in the chapter How To Get Found by Your Perfect Customers with Local SEO, Part 1).

How Jane Finds the Best Chinese Restaurants

Here's how a typical customer journey might look like for a brick-and-mortar business, in this case, a restaurant.

Jane thinks, "I'm hungry for Chinese food." She pulls out her smartphone, opens a browser, and searches Google for "Best Chinese restaurants near me open now."

She chooses the Google Maps result with the highest review average, taps on the result, browses through photos, and thinks the restaurant looks pretty good.

Jane taps on the website link, reviews the menu, and sees the *subgum lo mein* she's been hankering for. She then taps the button for directions, opens Google Maps again, and heads toward the restaurant. She enjoys the meal and then goes home to take a nap and watch *Real Housewives of Detroit*, not on the TV but the phone.

Her path to purchase using her smartphone looks like this:

> *Mobile Search > Google Listing / Website / Directories > Looks at Photos > Reads Reviews > Gets Directions > Goes to Restaurant > Makes a Purchase.*

Within a matter of minutes, Jane used a search engine, Google Maps, read some reviews, visited the website, looked at food photography, and made a decision — all from her mobile phone.

She didn't spend time checking for hours of operation or looking around for the best restaurant. She simply searched with "best" at the beginning of her query, and Google automatically sorted the results based on which restaurants had the highest ratings and that were open now and nearby. Boom shakalaka!

It's possible that Jane could have seen a Facebook promotion or AdWords ad in Google Maps. Or, perhaps, she received a coupon, had she been a customer.

Not unlike Jane, regardless of the path they take to get to your place of business, it's very likely that your customers will interact with several different forms of digital marketing media along the way and, often, use their phone to make the entire journey. Be sure to have a fully mobile-friendly presence, strong reviews, and complete listing information on not only your website but also on all the directories and review sites your customers might use along their path to do business with you.

How Mobile Has Changed Everything Forever

People who have smartphones use them constantly. It's kind of a problem. In fact, there is a new psychological condition called nomophobia (an abbreviation for "no-mobile-phone phobia") for the fear that people experience when they are away from their phone or without cell coverage. I'll bet that you are holding your smartphone right now... or at least thinking about it. Just put it down and read this book for a few minutes, please.

People will use their smartphones to interact with your brand to:

- Read reviews of your business on directories like Google Maps, Yelp, Facebook, and Foursquare;

- Check out your website;

- Follow and interact with you on social networks such as Facebook, Twitter, Instagram, SnapChat, and others;

- Get directions to your store and see store hours using Apple Maps or Google Maps (where they'll also see reviews);

- Read your email newsletters.

Whether you personally search for local businesses on your smartphone or not doesn't matter. Most of your consumers will, and it's time to adapt to the new era of local business commerce. The rest of the book will help you understand how to prioritize your marketing efforts to get the best results possible.

Key Takeaways From How Today's Consumers Find Local Businesses

- The way people research purchasing decisions for local businesses is increasingly influenced by the information they find on their smartphones.

- Consumers use search engines, company websites, and social media, respectively, to find local businesses.

- Map out your customer buyer journey to plan out marketing content at various milestones in their process of doing business with you.

- All the media encountered along your customer journey (website, online reservations, email, videos) must be 100% mobile-friendly and easy to use on a smartphone.

2

THE FOUNDATION OF DIGITAL MARKETING FOR LOCAL BUSINESSES

"You can't build a great building
on a weak foundation."

- Gordon B. Hinckley

Growing your business with digital marketing is a lot like building a house. As with any structure, you must have a strong foundation before you can get to tasks like painting your walls or choosing matching kitchen appliances.

Similarly, with digital marketing,
once your foundational elements
are solid, you can really scale
with other aspects of
digital marketing, such as
email marketing, social media,
and online advertising.
If you skip building the foundation,
however, the structure will crumble.

Here is a case in point: To get traffic and sales quickly, many businesses take shortcuts by investing a lot of money in Google Adwords or Facebook ads, which can work well while the ads are running. But once the ads stop running, the customers stop coming. That's not what building a strong foundation is all about.

By investing in your marketing using the strategy and tactics I teach in this book, however, you will build online equity gradually over time. Your online presence will grow organically in a way that generates leads for your business with significantly less ongoing investment than a purely paid traffic approach possibly could.

In the chapter "How Today's Consumers Find Local Businesses," I reference a study by the Local Search Association — the "Digital Consumer Study" — which showed that consumers find local businesses through search engines, their company website, and social media before anything else. The findings of that study complement my nine years of experience in helping over 300 local businesses with digital marketing. That's why branding, website development, and local SEO make up the foundational layers of what I refer to as my digital marketing pyramid.

Digital Marketing Foundational Elements

We'll dive deeper into each of the elements listed below in the following chapters, but here is a quick overview of the foundational elements of local business digital marketing in their respective order:

1. Branding
2. Website
3. Local SEO
4. Email Marketing
5. Social Media
6. Online Advertising

Branding

Your branding will be used throughout the entire customer journey in all of your marketing. Before you begin creating a website or social media content, it's important to have a solid message, clear values, logo, tagline, colors, and brand image to carry throughout all of your marketing.

While using sites like 99designs.com or fiverr.com can get you some pretty decent graphics for your social media posts, I recommend working with a professional marketer who truly understands branding and messaging to develop your assets to get the best lifetime value from them. Having a skimpy-looking logo may sway people away from your business once they find you, rather than attract them to it.

Website

Having a solid website is critical to your success as a local business. Not only does your website impact how you rank in search engines, it can provide information for potential customers and lead them into your sales process through contact forms, directions, and other calls to action.

Local SEO

Local SEO, which is heavily related to your website, is increasingly important as more and more people are searching for local businesses on their mobile devices. From finding your store hours to getting directions to reading reviews, local SEO should be a critical part of your digital marketing plan.

Email Marketing

Email marketing continues to be one of the most cost-effective forms of digital marketing. You can use it to acquire new customers but, more importantly, to retain existing customers and generate repeat business.

Social Media

Social media is a great way to connect with customers, foster repeat business, and interact directly with customers who are providing feedback on social channels.

Online Advertising

Online advertising, with Facebook ads and Google AdWords, can be a great way to generate customers on demand once you have the foundational elements of your digital marketing in place.

I strongly recommend that you invest in your marketing in the order I have outlined above. Doing so will ensure your digital marketing "house" remains strong for years to come.

Other Foundational Elements

Aside from digital marketing, there are other elements that contribute to building a strong foundation and becoming a thriving local brand. They include excellence in customer service, a profitable location or service area, active community involvement, and having a good level of hustle.

Building on those elements, you must also have a:

- Business vision, mission, and purpose;

- Customer relationship management system (CRM) to organize and keep track of your customers;

- Reliable point of sale system (POS) and credit card processing software;

- Sales process and salespeople;

- Accounting software and a process to keep your books straight;

- Customer service process and people to take care of customers;

- Strong offering, pricing model, and attractive business model;

- Level of marketing and operational automation.

Key Takeaways From The Foundation Of Digital Marketing For Local Businesses

- Digital marketing for local businesses is the sum of many separate but related elements.

- Build your marketing with a solid foundation upon which you can grow.

- Don't skip any of the foundational elements when creating your digital marketing.

- Focus your time, energy, and budget first on the bottom three layers of the pyramid and gradually work your way up.

- Remember that local business foundation building isn't limited to digital channels; other "offline" elements are equally important.

3

LAY THE FOUNDATION FOR GROWTH WITH STRONG BRANDING

"You can't make a record
if you ain't got nothin' to say."

- Willie Nelson

Branding, a term that has its etymology in farming, marking animals with a burn as a way of identifying them, is the necessary foundation upon which local businesses engage in marketing.

There are a lot of ways of defining branding where marketing is concerned. Here's mine:

> Branding is identifying and
> communicating your company's
> core values to distinguish
> your business from others.

What's the difference between branding and marketing? Branding is strategic; marketing is tactical.

What Do You Stand For?

In most markets, there are several companies offering similar products and services as you. In most urban and suburban cities in America, there are at least a couple dozen HVAC contractors, home repair companies, dentists, lawyers, Pilates studios, yoga studios, locksmiths, therapists, and real estate agents. In my case, there are over 200 marketing companies in the Boulder area.

> What really makes a brand
> is *the way* they do things.
> It's *the way they do things* that creates
> a culture and attracts similar people.
> *The way* we do things and what we
> stand for make up our core values.

When I talk about core values, I don't care about what you scribbled down on your business plan ten years ago that you never look at. I'm talking about *what's important to you in how you treat people and how you work. Branding is initially an extension of the founder's core beliefs and values.*

It took me a long time to finally clarify in writing what my own core values were, but once I did, it felt so good. These are the values that we'd been operating by all along, and after reading the book *Traction* by Gino Wickman[1], writing them down in a brainstorming session with Ramblin Jackson COO Leah Leaves was exhilarating.

Ramblin Jackson's Core Values

1. Be On-time and Prepared to Add Value
2. Craftsmanship in Life & Work, Especially on Fridays
3. Create Profit and Results with Integrity

4. Grow or Die
5. Be Human (& Pick Up the Damn Phone)
6. Professional
7. Raise the Stakes

We make our core values a part of everyday operation, from how we greet customers to how we interview, hire, and manage our staff. We even have a Beef Jerky Club where we promise to be On-Time and Prepared To Add Value to all meetings. If we're ever late, we send our clients beef jerky (or deluxe almonds if they're not meat-eaters) in the mail as an apology.

See if you qualify to join my
Beef Jerky Club at
ramblinjackson.com/jerky/

When you have your core values clearly identified, communicating your branding becomes so much easier.

Your Branding Will Be Seen Everywhere and Influence Every Sale, for Better or Worse

The words, colors, and imagery you use in your logo, business cards, vehicle wraps, social media icons, letterhead, signage, menus, uniforms, promotional items, and anything else that someone might possibly see has a profound impact on people's perception of your business's professionalism and capabilities.

Many companies overlook *what they are actually communicating in branding* and jump straight to sites like 99Designs.com, an online graphic design marketplace, to get a logo quickly and cheaply. While services like 99Designs can be useful once you have true branding in place, opting for cheap logo design may, in the long run, cost you more than you save.

Branding is really about understanding the emotional reasons that motivate someone to choose your product or service over another.

From a digital marketing standpoint, strong branding is critical for cutting through the noise of crowded Facebook newsfeeds, cluttered email inboxes, and skeezy DIY websites to, ultimately, attracting the right customers who will create profit for your business.

Here are a handful of the places people will encounter your branding in your digital marketing:

- Your social media icons and profile pictures;

- Your email newsletters.(Will people instantly recognize your brand and trust your email or quickly mark it as spam and unsubscribe?);

- Your website;

- Your mobile app, if you have one.

All Sales Are Motivated by Avoidance of Pain

All sales are motivated by avoiding pain, whether it's a physical pain, emotional pain... or even a broken window pane if you are a window replacement contractor!

Usually, there's an event that triggers somebody to think, "Oh, I might need a new glass window" or "I need *whatever it is your company offers.*" Think about those triggering events and how they may cause the person to reach out to friends, ask for a referral, and, likely, look online to find a solution.

If you write down — on a big-ass whiteboard or piece of paper — the events that trigger the pains your business solves, you can create a killer list of blog posts, landing pages, videos, and email content ideas that can help attract a potential customer and let them know.

What do people google when they have the pain that you solve?

What subject line would they absolutely open if they received an email from you?

Here's a copywriting tip I learned from my one of my business coaches, Wayne Herring. (www.herringcoach.com)

Copywriting Tip: Write down on Post-It notes with a medium-point Sharpie the sales objections and pains you uncover during your sales calls with prospects. Keep these notes and after a few weeks or months you'll have a very clear understanding of the actual pains you solve and a great set of ideas for blog posts and ideas.

A marketer whose content I consume almost religiously is Jason Swenk, a business coach who sold a $12,000,000 advertising agency and now coaches guys like me to run better digital agencies.

Why do I consume all of his content? Because Jason Swenk *markets exclusively to solving the pains that a digital agency owner faces.* (He also literally owns his own mountain in Colorado and has been extremely successful!) When I get an email or YouTube notification from Jason Swenk, you can bet the content answers a real pain or problem that I am likely dealing with at this moment. It's not the normal B.S. about "how to run a better small business," it's about the *specific* real pains that have literally kept me up at night when I'm stressed about something in my business. *How can you do that for YOUR customer?*

(Wayne and Jason are two of my favorite business coaches. Hear Jason's podcast interview with Wayne about How to Find and Train an Agency Sales Rockstar at www.jasonswenk.com/agency-sales/)

What Fears Do Consumers Have of Your Industry?

Let's say that you've clearly identified your prospect's pain (and maybe you can even solve it and they know it), what are the fears, doubts, and uncertainties that they would have that might prevent them from working with you or your industry? Write these down and be aware of them — and overcome them with your branding and marketing.

Here are some examples of stories people see in the news that make them afraid of local home repair or landscape companies.

What are the fears people may have of your industry?

How effectively does your online branding — your website, videos, and reviews — overcome those fears to make your customer trust you?

If your customer fears real stories like the ones above, the need for strong branding and marketing is even greater.

The same goes for recruiting employees. Is your industry notorious for cheap employers who buy bad equipment that poops out on the jobsite, leaving their hourly employees without work? Could an inspiring team photo of your whole crew wearing uniforms in front of quality gear help inspire a potential employee that you are clearly a better employer than the last guy? Heck yeah!

5 Branding Questions to Answer Before You Create Marketing Materials

Pour a cup of coffee and grab a pen and a piece of paper. Turn off your phone and computer. Handwrite the answers to these questions. Go ahead and *write in this book*. I'd be honored if you did.

1. What are the core values of your company?

2. What do customers HATE about your industry? What are they afraid could possibly go wrong with you? What do you do better than your competition on industry to alleviate the fears people have?

3. What's the biggest pain or problem you solve for your customers, and how does it change their life when you solve it?

4. What can you guarantee?

5. How do you want people to <u>feel</u> when they have a good experience with your company?

Now, take a step back and look at your website... at your marketing materials. *Are the answers you wrote down clear in your marketing materials?*

Crafting a Unique Selling Proposition to Attract the Best Customers

There are a lot of definitions of Unique Selling Propositions (USP) or unique sales positions, but let's not over complicate it. Essentially, what is it you offer that makes you different? In crowded markets this is even more imperative.

Once you've identified what your clients hate — what drives them nuts, what are they afraid of, and what are YOUR values — you can craft an irresistible USP to help attract the best customers and generate the most profit.

Here are a few examples of clients I've worked with who have USPs that help them stand out in their local market. You'll find that, in all cases, there is a deep emotional reason that truly drives them — not just stuff some marketing guy came up with in a meeting one day.

The Little Yoga Studio
www.littleyogastudio.com

What Customers Hate	Unique Selling Proposition
Overly "spiritual" yoga studios; overpriced drop-in rates trying to get you to buy a membership; fancy showers; real estate driving up price	High Quality Yoga without the B.S. $10 Drop-Ins

ProMaster Handyman & Home Repair of Cincinnati
www.mastermylist.com

What Customers Hate	Unique Selling Proposition
Shady dudes who show up late, make a big mess, and aren't respectful of their home	On-time & Family-friendly

Superscape Landscape
www.superscapelandscape.com

What Customers Hate	Unique Selling Proposition
Noisy, gas-guzzling lawn care companies	Cape Cod's Environmentally-friendly Lawn Care

Call Rich Bradley from Superscape Landscape and ask him how he feels about the environmental impact of gas-powered lawn mowers vs. battery-powered ones. Follow him at the GIE+ EXPO, the world's largest landscape conference, to the trade show booth of Greenworks, the battery-powered equipment provider where he buys his gear. He's like a kid in a candy store.

Ask Kelly Elle Kentworthy from the Little Yoga Studio how she feels about preachy yoga studios with expensive memberships and extensive contracts.

Call Don Kennedy from ProMaster Handyman and Home Repair of Cincinnati and ask him how he feels about contractors who use drugs and show up late to jobs.

Call me on the telephone sometime — (303) 544-2125 — and ask me how I feel about marketing companies who build websites that get hacked or "SEO companies" that don't share their keyword research with their clients.

You'll find that each of those people is seriously fired up and hell bent on doing things a certain way. THAT is their brand.

Your branding is an extension of YOUR values and a solution to your customer's pains. By focusing your USP as a solution to your prospect's biggest pain and frustrations, you're able to charge more, increase profits, and work with higher quality customers.

Kudos to The Little Yoga Studio for winning Best Yoga Studio in Boulder two times (out of 40+ studios in Boulder!) and ProMaster Handyman & Home Repair of Cincinnati for winning the Better Business Bureau Torch Award two times as well. You can bet that those businesses dedication to quality and their USP (and a little help from some marketing guy in Boulder) has paid off.

Examples of Bad Branding in Local Business and Wasted Real Estate

For brick-and-mortar businesses, signage and storefront presentation is an important part of communicating your branding. It never ceases to amaze me how many tens of thousands of dollars -- sometimes per MONTH -- these companies will spend to have a prime storefront location with lots of foot or vehicular traffic, only to waste it with a lack of branding.

McDonald's vs. Burger King
On 28th Street in Boulder

28th Street in Boulder, Colorado, is prime real estate. On one side are several blocks of high-end, highly-trafficked strip malls with stores like REI and Bed, Bath and Beyond.

On the other side is the 29th Street Mall, which has tons of stores, including Trader Joe's, Target, Men's Warehouse, The Home Depot, The Mac Store, The North Face, Mad Greens, and others.

Thousands of people drive through there every day as it leads to Highway 36 towards Denver to the south and to Longmont in the north. Again, prime real estate.

In the middle of the mall are McDonald's and Burger King — right next to each other.

Here are some photos of the back end of the two restaurants from the street that runs through the 29th Street Mall.

From behind, I wouldn't know what this business is or what it offers, particularly if I hadn't seen the front of the building. There is a low sign that says "drive-thru" so I can assume that it's some kind of fast food restaurant. Otherwise, there is no mention of the word Burger King. At all. (That is with the exception of a tiny logo on a temporary flabby sign staked into the ground promoting a special.)

Other brand "fails" include:

- The red and yellow used in the trim of the building does not match any of the colors in their logo;

- The "drive-thru" sign does not have any mention of what it is for;

- The building clearly hasn't been updated in at least 15 years;

- The menu sign is kind of ramshackle looking, with one of the panels crooked.

What an utter waste of real estate. How many thousands of people drive past that every single day and don't know what it is?

Contrast that with the view of McDonald's, just 10 yards away:

- The McDonald's Golden Arches are clearly visible everywhere;

- The word "McDonald's" can be seen on each side of the building, along with other signage;

- The exterior of the building, which was recently remodeled, includes a cool, modern-looking design and a neat wood feature that gives it kind of a healthy vibe;

- The signs are well lit, legible, and branded.

Notice how the parking lot is full and that there are two drive-thru lanes, which are also full. McDonald's is obviously killing it here.

If you look at the Google trends for McDonald's versus Burger King, it's apparent that there are at least 40% more searches for McDonald's. There are a number of factors that can influence this, including their advertising budget, but it is clear that more people search for the brand McDonald's than Burger King.

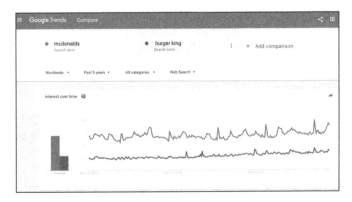

Let's take a look at the signage for a local business that is probably more like yours.

The Kitchen and Bath Shop in Boulder

Here is a photo of a kitchen and bath store, also in Boulder, taken by my friend Jeffrey Magner. It is located in the Village Shopping Center, a strip mall that has other businesses, restaurants, and high-traffic places. The rent is astronomical.

Here is a view from less than 50 feet away. It's the business in the middle with the neon signs. What is this business? What does it sell?

How much money is wasted paying up the wazoo to rent the space where thousands of potential customers will walk past it each week only to have a lack of clear signage that communicates what it does?

The Refrigerator Delivery That Wasn't Very Cool

One time, the refrigerator at the house my wife and I rented needed to be replaced. Our landlords, who are wonderful people and also very frugal, decided to get a refurbished refrigerator from a local business about thirty minutes from where we lived.

They let us know the refrigerator would be delivered on a particular date and time by a certain company. One of the first things my wife and I did was Google the company's name to read the customer reviews. Here's what we found:

Google My Business

1.7 ★★ ★ ★ ★   56 Google reviews
Appliance repair service in Longmont, Colorado

Yelp

https://www.yelp.com › Shopping › Home & Garden › Appliances ▾
★★ ★ ★ ★ Rating: 1.6 - 16 reviews · Price range: $$

YellowPages

www.yellowpages.com › Used Major Appliances near Longmont, CO ▾
★★★ ★ ★ Rating: 2.5 - 5 reviews

As you can see, their reviews are atrocious. They have a 1.7 rating on Google and dozens of reviews describe the terrible experience people have had with the staff, late appointments, and faulty equipment.

Their website has no content on the about page...
no logo... no tagline... no staff photos or bios...
nothing. Not even the owner of the company was
mentioned on the website. It's a quick and dirty
GoDaddy website with little thought or care given.

We shared our concern with the landlord, who went
to the business and talked with the owner of the
company. The owner assured our landlord that
things would go smoothly and that they were
aware of the bad reviews. We were somewhat
comforted by this but still quite skeptical.

They were scheduled to deliver the refrigerator
between 1 and 4 p.m. on a Thursday. I decided to
work from home that day so I could be there during
the delivery (*in case sketchy dudes show up to the
house, I thought*). I am so glad that I made that
choice.

By the time 4:30 rolled around and they had not
arrived, I texted our landlord who called the
delivery company who said they would be there a
little closer to 5:00... and then 5:30... and then
6:00. We continued to text the landlord who again
called, only to learn that "something unexpected
happened."

We then called the company to let them know that
seven o'clock was the absolute latest they could
show up as we put our kids down for bed at 7:30
p.m. We were told they would be there by then.

I put my son to bed, and just as I was leaving his bedroom, heard a knock at the door. By then, it was 7:50 p.m.

When I opened the door, there were two guys wearing, not uniforms with the company's logo and colors, but big baggy black jeans and enormous hoodies.

They grumbled the name of their company and their first names and proceeded to, very noisily, move our old refrigerator out of the house and the new one in. One of them was very angry and mumbled something about having to work late two days before Christmas.

They brought an old refrigerator from off a trailer pulled by a car, neither of which had any branding either.

> Late delivery by creepy
> dudes IS their brand.
> That's exactly what they do!
> No wonder they lack the basics of
> a logo, vehicle wraps,
> a quality website, reviews, etc.

Contrast that with this example of ProMaster Handyman & Home Repair of Cincinnati, a home service company that puts great emphasis on brand-building.

How ProMaster Handyman & Home Repair of Cincinnati Won the Better Business Bureau Torch Award — Twice

One of my favorite clients — Don Kennedy, owner of ProMaster Handyman & Home Repair of Cincinnati, Ohio — found my digital agency, Ramblin Jackson, as a result of a comment on a popular local SEO blog post. Over the years, Don and I have become close friends and enjoy not only working together, but also talking about sales, marketing, management, business, leadership, and even things like parenting, homeschooling, and life in general.

Following years of a mostly remote relationship over the phone, email, and text messaging, Don flew out to Colorado to visit me for a half day of sales and marketing brainstorming that included him sharing his branding philosophy and strategy. While we had talked about it before, I never fully appreciated his approach to branding until I had the experience with the shady delivery company.

ProMaster is "on time and family friendly." They are also "the home repair heroes." They schedule specific appointment times and show up on time every time, in uniform, in a beautifully-branded vehicle. Customers can even request specific craftsman, all of whom have bios and photos on the company website, accompanied by user reviews and ratings.

Their brand is:

- Masculine;

- On-time and family-friendly;

- Clean, uniformed, and professional.

Don came to me with a complex local SEO issue, which we solved. Over the years of doing his search engine optimization and online advertising, he tripled his lead generation. This resulted in a huge increase in revenue, and I was excited to be working with Don when he passed the million-dollar milestone.

But it wasn't just the fact we increased Don's rankings in Google that factored into his success. (We also coached him on things like collecting reviews on Google and his lead-qualifying website.) Rather, it is the solid brand foundation he has built over time that serves as the main contributor.

Everything about Promaster's branding, from its logo to the business cards, uniforms, signage, and vehicle wraps, is designed to communicate their company values and create a positive emotional reaction from prospective clients — something the refrigerator guys will never experience!

As these two examples illustrate, branding isn't just about logos and colors but also customer service, which contributes to the customer's impression of brand value. Poor customer service creates a negative impression of the brand just as good customer service creates a favorable one.

Watch the interview with Don to find out how he tripled his lead generation in one year through his local SEO at ramblinjackson.com/donkennedy/

Key Takeaways From Laying The Foundation For Growth With Strong Branding

- Successful branding is much more than just your logo and colors.

- Your branding will be seen everywhere and influence every sale, for better or worse.

- Create your Unique Selling Proposition (USP) around solving the pains and fears your clients have and you will WIN.

- Create your branding with your customers' emotional state in mind.

- Leverage your branding everywhere your customers will interact with your company.

4

DISQUALIFY BAD PROSPECTS WITH PROFESSIONAL WEBSITE DESIGN

"Design is not just what it looks like and how it feels. Design is how it works."

- Steve Jobs

Many local business owners vastly underestimate the impact their website can have on their sales. This chapter will help you see what your website could and should accomplish for your business, so you can make more informed decisions about how your site is built, which software you will use, and who you will hire to design it.

The Job of Your Website Is to Fuel Sales, Not Be a Brochure

Your website has a very important job to do. It is not just a "brochure," like many people think of them. Instead, it can become your company's best salesperson. Your website is open 24/7/365, delivers a consistent sales message, educates and informs prospects, knows everything about your business, and can help attract qualified prospects and weed out the bad ones through strong copy.

Here are some specific responsibilities your website should perform:

- Establish trust and legitimacy of your company to prospective customers;

- Help your business get found in search engines;

- Communicate key information such as store hours, directions, services offered, portfolio photographs, menus, goods sold, and more;

- Persuade viewers that you are worth doing business with;

- Qualify prospects;

- DISqualify BAD prospects to stop them from wasting your time;

- Convert visitors into phone calls, directions to your business, leads through a contact form, or subscribers to your email newsletter, blog, or landing page;

- Provide a place for your company to publish content you can share via social media and email.

Your Website Must Be Able to Grow with Your Business

Your website must be able to perform new duties as your business grows. For example, you may adopt a new online registration program, point of sale or customer relationship management system, calendar tool, or ecommerce shopping cart. When choosing a content management system (CMS), it's important that you select one that can grow with you over time.

Don't Shortchange Yourself with a Cheap Website CMS

A cheap out-of-the-box do-it-yourself website builder such as GoDaddy, Weebly, Wix, or SquareSpace may be a good fit in the very early stages of your business, if you're in a low competition market, or if your income potential is less than $100,000 per year.

However, platforms such as these can come with serious restrictions in terms of search engine optimization (SEO), functionality, integration, and design — factors that can cost you much more than you're saving due to missed opportunity and future website redesign expenses, and also a lack of sales due to a perceived lower quality or expertise.

While not all are inherently flawed, take the time to thoroughly research your options and determine what you want your website to accomplish before making your choice.

Things to Consider When Choosing Your Website Content Management System (CMS)

SEO

Many website CMS vendors have a templated drag-and-drop website builder, which can be very easy to use and appeal to a small business owner on a limited budget, but may compromise SEO.

For instance, at the time of this writing (March 2018), you cannot add schema to Wix websites. We'll discuss schema in greater detail in the chapter on Local SEO, but it is, essentially, code that you add to your website to help your business display better in search results. In a competitive market, having schema on your site could make the difference between someone clicking to your site and doing business with you versus a competitor.

Integration

Another important factor when selecting your website CMS is its ability to integrate with other software programs.

Does the website need to integrate with your CRM, point of sale, or inventory management system, or with your email, automation, or other marketing programs? Vet your website software integrations and compare them against the programs you're using or those you may use in the future.

Site Speed

As consumers become more dependent on smartphones, their patience for slow-loading sites decreases. They want the site to load fast, without delay.

Site speed is not only a factor in Google's search algorithm but, more importantly, in people's decision to use your website, or not.

Many of the out-of-the-box template websites not only load slowly but, worse, there's often nothing you can do to improve their load speed. You're stuck with a slow-loading website on a server you don't control with a thousand other cheap template websites that also run as slow as mud. Awesome. How much does that site actually cost you when people are leaving it and you're not ranking in Google?

Design and Other Customization

Design matters. A lot. Design is especially important if your company sells a high-dollar item in a competitive market, such as landscaping, remodeling, or legal services. Therefore, when choosing your website platform, consider how much control over the design you'd like to have.

To Command Higher Prices, You Must Look the Best

If your online marketing is bringing in pain-in-the-ass prospects with no budget, it could be the fault of your website.

Cheap-Looking Design
Brings In Cheap Customers

This is especially true if you sell a *design* service, such as landscape design, custom jewelry, or kitchen/bath/home remodeling. People are hiring you to make their home or personal appearance look better. If your website doesn't inspire confidence that you have design skills, you're toast.

Similarly, if you *look cheap* and someone thinks "Oh, good, they look cheap!" you're going to have a lot of no-good tire-kickin' yellow-bellied price shoppers eating up your time "collecting some quotes."

If you want to command higher prices and win bigger jobs, you need to look the part *online* for people to consider calling you.

Design's Influence in Purchasing Decisions

Roughly 7 in 10 adults in the U.S. would choose a product or service over its competition based on good design, according to Adobe's State of Create report[1], which referenced a survey of more than 5,000 adults in 2016. Also, consumers will decide within 1/20 to 1/50th of a second if a website is beautiful, reported a 2012 Google study[2].

Those statistics are certainly eye-opening, but let's take a look at what they meant for a real small business owner.

How Professional Web Design Saved Jill Yellico's Fledgling Business

Jill Yellico bought Discovery Kids at Rockrimmon, a daycare center in Colorado Springs, Colorado. The business was really struggling, and Jill bought it from the original owner for a steal, thinking she could quickly turn things around.

While Jill was able to shift a lot of the operational issues immediately, she found herself facing another challenge: the inability to get new customers.

When she came to Ramblin Jackson, Jill had an awful website. She had built it herself using Wix. I told her that, honestly, as a parent, I would not trust her business with my kids because the website was so bad that it gave me the impression her business was unprofessional and untrustworthy.

Not only that, she failed to rank in search engines for any of her target keywords — even really easy, low competition phrases like "daycare" + the name of her neighborhood.

We redesigned Jill's website to appear more professional, cleaned up her SEO, and optimized the new site. While it took several months for her rankings to increase, she saw immediate improvement in the conversion rate of site visitors into new enrollments once new people were finding her site.

Testimonial: The True Cost of Hiring an Amateur Web Designer

"It was certainly a challenge for us to make sure that we were recognized in our community. And that was one of our biggest challenges. We weren't getting tours, we are kind of off on a side street in the neighborhood which is good for a child care center, but we don't have the kind of exposure to the big city streets that you would have so people see you driving by. So, that was something that the website afforded us. As soon as our website was up and running we had tours almost every day and our enrollment jumped.

*"**Now, the website and SEO is all we need to do for marketing**. We used to take flyers around in the neighborhood, we don't do that at all anymore. We're almost too full enrollment, so we don't market when we're at full enrollment.*

"Previously we had a website that I designed myself through Wix.com, but I didn't understand how to get it fully optimized. The design was unprofessional, and customers couldn't find us in Google because I didn't have any of the settings setup correctly.

"I'd had some experience with desktop publishers, so I thought I could build my own website and I did with Wix. It wasn't a very good website, it wasn't inclusive of all our programs and all of the pictures that we could have, and you couldn't find us on Google.

"We hired Ramblin Jackson to do our SEO and build our website on WordPress, and now we are first or second for any Google search for daycare in our area, which is huge, and our website looks professional and it's interactive!

"The additional revenue that we got from the Ramblin Jackson enrollment certainly more than paid for the price that we paid for the website and I think that a professional website reflects on the

kind of business you run. It says something about the professionalism of the organization that you run as a whole.

"As a result of the website and SEO, our gross revenue has increased by 33%. It saved the business."

- Jill Yellico, Owner of Discovery Kids at Rockrimmon

Local Business Website Design Best Practices

Whether you decide to build your website yourself, hire a freelancer, or work with an agency, be sure to create of it from the perspective of a marketer, not merely a *designer*, and that you create a site that actually helps your customers do business with you versus just making something pretty.

Here are a handful of website design best practices for local businesses:

Make Your Website Header Immediately Helpful to Customers

Your website's header (the top part of the site) is extremely important in getting people to take action. For a local business with a physical location, it should include the phone number, address, and, ideally, a link to directions. For a service-based business whose physical location isn't as critical to sales but where phone calls are the

main goal, you should at least have the phone
number clearly visible and as a hot button on
mobile.

Here's the header Ramblin Jackson designed for
Cronin Jewelers, a custom jewelry shop in Boulder,
Colorado. On mobile, the phone number opens the
phone app on a smartphone. Tap the address and
Google Maps appears. The Contact Us button pulls
out a pop-up form, which customers can fill out to
request more information.

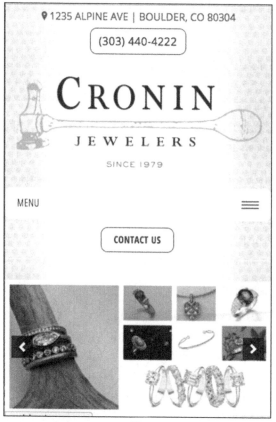

This functionality makes it very easy for customers to call Cronin or get directions, actions that can lead them into the store to make a purchase.

Here's another example of the desktop view of ProMaster Handyman and Home Repair of Cincinnati's website header, which is designed to help viewers search their website for content, call them, or "hail a hero" when they're ready.

Use Clear Calls to Action to Help People Take the Next Step in Doing Business with You

A call-to-action (CTA) is a button or link that you place on your website to drive visitors (and future customers) to take some action. A CTA can be an offer, highlight, or sign-up button. Whatever the option, it must provide some value to your customer.

People are lazy, so don't make them think. Instead, make it easy for them to know how to contact you with abundantly clear calls to action, such as a "Request A Quote," "Sign Up Now,", "Call Us Today," "Get Directions," and so forth.

Pinocchio's Italian Eatery in Brighton, Colorado, has a website that features a clearly-visible call to action button — "See Our Menu" — which links to the menu page. Similarly, if you shrink the site down on mobile, a button in the header says, "Get Directions."

Make the Experience Exceptional on Mobile

Optimize everything you do on your website for mobile — from the header to images to contact forms to newsletter signups. The site needs to load instantly, resize to fit smaller smartphone screens, and give your visitors a rich, useful experience. Failure to do so will cause them to quickly click away in favor of a competitor who has taken the time to optimize his site for mobile users.

Mobile surpassed desktop usage in the U.S. in 2014. Since then, Google has made several updates to its organic and advertising algorithms to head in a "mobile first" direction. In December of 2016, for example, Google began rolling out its own mobile index in which mobile-optimized sites outrank non-mobile sites. For local businesses, this is particularly important as people search for "near me" and for local businesses primarily from mobile.

Be sure that as you design your site, you test it on a variety of mobile devices and browser types to ensure it is easy for your customers to use.

Have Your Blog Integrated with Your Main Domain

If you are going to blog, and I suggest that most local businesses blog (see the Social Media chapter for more info), make it part of your main website, (i.e., bobskaratedojo.com/blog/) instead of using an external service such as bobskaratedojo.wordpress.com. Here are a few reasons why:

- **Branding** - You want to establish and promote *your* brand, not wordpress.com or some other blog service;

- **SEO** - By integrating your blog into your domain, you'll enjoy greater SEO benefits, such as customizing the SEO settings over the individual post and providing relevant redirections. Also, it will benefit your domain instead of wordpress.com's when other websites link to your blog post,

- **Ownership** - You don't own wordpress.com. It could go down and disappear with all of your blog posts. By self-hosting, you have better control over your posts long-term

Make Your Site Load Speed As Fast As Lightning

By golly, it better load fast. Forget about the SEO implications — *humans*, your customers, hate slow-loading sites. Remember how people decide in 1/50 of a second if a site is beautiful or not? What will they think if it takes five seconds to load? Probably not much — because they won't be there!

Check out Google's PageSpeed Insights to see how your site stacks up and get ideas for what you can improve. www.developers.google.com/speed/pagespeed/insights/

Choose Quality Website Hosting

One thing that really drives me nuts is when businesses invest thousands of dollars in designing, developing, and optimizing their website, only to skimp on hosting to save $100 a year or whatever.

What many business owners don't know is that the reason website hosting is so inexpensive is because their site is on the same server as potentially thousands of others, some containing content that might best be described as "sleazy." If one or more of those receives higher than normal traffic, the rest may load slowly due to resources being allocated to the high-traffic site.

When choosing a host, consider the following:

- **Security and Backups** - Does the host offer website security or backups? According to Google Search Console (formerly Webmaster Tools)[3], website hacking increased 180% in 2015. What happens if the site gets hacked? Anything? Or is it entirely gone?

- **Site Load Speed** - Does the host offer any site load speed enhancement opportunities, like Content Delivery Network (CDN), which is a service that can help the static content on your site (images, CSS, Javascript) load much more quickly? How many other sites are hosted on the server?

- **Customer Support** - Can you chat, email, or talk on the phone with someone 24/7 or are business hours limited? How responsive and helpful is the support team when you need them?

For WordPress website hosting, I recommend WP Engine. It is diesel! The customer support team wins awards nearly every year, sites are backed up every single day, and, if one is hacked, it gets fixed for free. WP Engine is the best by far.

(For a special rate on WP Engine hosting, visit www.bit.ly/wpenginejack)

Show Them the Experience Your Company Offers Through Great Photography

An important aspect of SEO, social media, and website design is having high-quality photographs that show people what it's like to work with you. Humans are visual creatures. They perceive a lot about you and your business by how you present yourself visually on your site.

For restaurants, excellent food photography and well-lit interior and exterior photographs can inspire people to pay a visit.

For landscapers, people really want to see what you can do, so schedule a professional photoshoot at the end of your projects and get some behind the scenes photos along the way for use on social media. They are hiring you to make their landscape beautiful — so inspire them with images of what's possible!

For service businesses, doctors, dentists, lawyers, or any company where employees will be interfacing with clients, having great team headshots and photographs can add a high level of credibility.

Photography Tip: Shoot all of your team headshots on the same background with the same camera.

The Eldorado Retina Associates' website is an example of this in action. Doesn't the staff look professional and trustworthy?

Cheryl Fehr – Front Office Coordinator
Cheryl is a long time resident of Colorado, a past preschool teacher and leader of several groups. She has taught 4-H and Sunday school. Cheryl enjoys flying with her husband, being with family & friends, reading, arts & crafts. She joined Eldorado Retina Associates in 2010.

Lauren Fox – Clinical Coordinator & Back Office Manager
Lauren, moved to Colorado in 2001 and graduated from University of Colorado Denver. She enjoys running, biking, hiking, cooking, time with family & friends. Lauren joined Eldorado Retina Associates in 2001.

Rebecca Larson – Front Office Manager & Head Photographer
Rebecca moved from California to Colorado in 1999. We consider her to be a world-class ophthalmic photographer. Rebecca enjoys the outdoors, camping, traveling, photography and painting. Rebecca started at Eldorado Retina Associates in 2007, and in 2008 began to study ophthalmic photography.

These days, with great cameras on smartphones and more affordable DSLR cameras, it seems anyone could be a photographer. While you can certainly DIY and do a pretty decent job, it's worth investing in professional photography, at least at the start so you have your best image forward on your website and directory listings. You can get a lot of use out of high-quality photos when you add them to your Google listing, Yelp, Facebook page, and other sites.

Page Load Speed Tip: When uploading photos to your website, optimize the image size so they don't bog down your site load speeds.

Write Quality Content

Remember the job I said your website needs to do? A lot of the selling, persuasion, and value-building will be done through copywriting. Have high-quality copy on your site to educate viewers about your business, its products and services, and the benefits of becoming a customer. See the "How To Develop Your On-Page SEO Strategy Page-by-Page" section of chapter six of this book for more information about writing for the web.

Why I Love WordPress

While there are many different content management systems available, there is one that I personally use and recommend to clients: WordPress.

Wordpress.com started out as blogging software. *Wordpress.org* is a CMS with which you can build a fully-customized website.

The reasons I like WordPress are numerous: The platform is scalable, can integrate with just about any software program a small business might use, is fully customizable from a design standpoint, has enormous search engine optimization benefits, and is the most used content management system in the world, currently powering about 25% of the web.

Although WordPress sites offer many benefits, be careful that the person developing your website builds it in a way that it works with future software updates. It's important to choose a theme and plugins that are maintained and updated regularly to keep your site efficient and secure. Poorly designed websites using old themes and plugins can be hacked. In general, buying a theme that uses a framework is better than using a theme without a framework.

At Ramblin Jackson, we use a WordPress framework called Genesis, which ensures that we can update our sites in the future. There are numerous out-of-the-box themes to choose from or our developers can customize a site for you.

How One Landscaper Uses His Website to Stand Out from Chuck-In-A-Truck Competitors

Clay Brooks needed a way to weed out every Tom, Dick and Harry who called with a $500 budget to fill in a hole in their yard. Those bad prospects ate up Clay's most limited resource: his time. His old website didn't position him as a high-end landscaper. Now, his new website shows off the design/build projects and *disqualifies the bad customers from even calling him* so he <u>keeps his pipeline full of qualified leads</u> with $50,000+ projects.

"We now stand out from Joe Blow landscaper in a truck and get the right leads calling us "

Clay Brooks
The Landscaping Company

See an interview with Clay at
ramblinjackson.com/claybrooks/

Key Takeaways From Disqualify Bad Prospects With Professional Website Design

- The job of your website is to facilitate sales, not be a brochure, so make it your best salesperson.

- Don't shortchange yourself by using a cheap website CMS.

- Good design influences consumer purchase decisions.

- Use clear calls to action to help visitors take the next step in the purchase path.

- Make the site experience exceptional on mobile.

- Integrate the blog within your main domain.

- Make your site load speed as fast as lightning.

- Choose quality website hosting.

- Use professional photography.

- Write quality website content.

5

HOW TO GET FOUND BY YOUR PERFECT CUSTOMERS WITH LOCAL SEO PART 1

"The difference between the almost right word and the right word is really a large matter — it's the difference between the lightning bug and the lightning."

- Mark Twain

Did you know that 76% of people who search on their smartphones for something nearby visit a business within a day, and 28% of those searches result in a purchase? To reap the benefits your business needs to get found ahead of your competitors in search engines like Google, Bing, Google Maps, and so on. To do that, you need Local SEO.

But what does "Local SEO" even mean?

While there is a whole lot more technical information you would need to know to *do* local SEO, which we'll cover in Part 2, my intent in this part is to educate you on the basics so you have enough of an understanding to have a conversation with your marketing team or an SEO company about what work needs to be done.

In this section, I'll show you how just one webpage generated over $200,000 of revenue for a Pilates studio in Denver, and how a local pizza joint that grosses over $4M lost 30% in revenue by making a common SEO mistake. There's a lot at stake here!

Even if you don't want to "do" SEO, you owe it to yourself to understand this information just as much as you need to understand your financial statements and tax deductions when talking with your accountant so you pay as little taxes as possible.

Key Terms: Demystifying the Jargon

There is a lot of SEO-related jargon and acronyms that can be helpful, but also distracting if you don't know what they mean. And, often, unethical SEO sales people will use such jargon to confuse small business owners.

If you're new to digital marketing, the sheer number of websites, social networks, and business acronyms you'll encounter can seem overwhelming — especially when it comes to SEO.

First, I'd like to offer a basic definition of "local SEO," so we're on the same page moving forward.

Throughout this chapter, and in other parts of the book, I will reference a company called Moz, a company based in Seattle, Washington, that creates marketing software used by hundreds of thousands of marketers around the world. They have an incredible online community of digital marketers, conferences, and products to help businesses improve their marketing.

Moz is regarded by members of the digital marketing community, including myself, as a top authority on the topic of SEO. At this time, I am not in any way affiliated with Moz, but I have been a user of their software, products, and community for over five years, and refer to them with great respect.

Here's how Moz defines **SEO** on its website:

> *"Short for search engine optimization, the process of increasing the number of visitors to a Web site by achieving high rank in the search results of a search engine. The higher a Web site ranks in the results of a search, the greater the chance that users will visit the site. It is common practice for Internet users to not click past the first few pages*

of search results, therefore high rank in SERPs is essential for obtaining traffic for a site. SEO helps to ensure that a site is accessible to a search engine and improves the chances that the site will be indexed and favorably ranked by the search engine."

Here's my definition of Local SEO:

*"**Local SEO is the process of helping a retail business**, service area business, or other company that has a geographic market get found online in the websites, directories, and search engines commonly used by consumers searching for a local business."*

Another way of defining Local SEO is a form of internet marketing that helps a local business get found by customers who search in search directories, social networks, maps, and applications using phrases such as "restaurants near me," "Chicago tire shops," "Dallas Dentists," or similar queries.

"SEO" can also refer to a person, such as myself, who does SEO work professionally. (i.e., "Bob is an SEO who specializes in health care businesses.")

If your company has a physical location that people need to go to for business to happen — a restaurant, office, clinic, or gym — or if you have a geographic area where you provide services, such as plumbing, home repair services, real estate, etc., then you would likely benefit from Local SEO.

Search Ranking

"Ranking" is the word used to refer to a business's position in the search engine results pages (SERPS) . A website in the first position would have a higher ranking than one in the ninth position, for example. One of the goals of SEO is to increase a business's ranking (as part of the bigger picture goal of getting more people finding you and contacting you to buy).

Search Query

A query is a question or phrase people would type or speak into a search engine or personal assistant.

Keyword

A keyword is a word or phrase with the terms people would search in their query.

Here's an example for a local business:

- Query: best chinese restaurants near me

- Keywords (bolded): best **chinese restaurants** near me

There are a lot of other definitions and related words, but this list should suffice for the purpose of this chapter. If business jargon really floats your boat and you want to geek out on more SEO jargon, check out the blog post, "A Complete Glossary of Essential SEO Jargon," on Moz's website.[1]

The Anatomy of Local Search Results

If you own a local business or work on its marketing in any capacity, it's important that you have at least a basic understanding of how search engines work and what devices your customers use. As technology and communication are constantly evolving, this can seem like a moving target as search engines like Google continually update their algorithms, feeds, and designs, and as new technology continues to come out.

At the time of this writing, here is how search results appear for the query, "cosmetic dentists denver co." I chose this query as an example because, having successfully marketed several dental practices, I know that it has high search volume, a decent amount of competition, and local intent.

Desktop Results

Here's what it looks like when I searched the query in Google's search engine from my browser on a laptop.

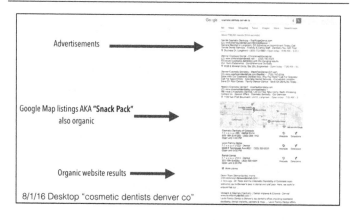

Advertisements

Google Map listings AKA **"Snack Pack"**
also organic

Organic website results

8/1/16 Desktop "cosmetic dentists denver co"

Paid Results: Google Adwords Advertisements

The top two listings have the word "Ad" next to them in a green font. Those businesses are paying to be there through Google Adwords, Google's paid advertising program.

Part of Google Adwords is Pay Per Click (PPC) , and businesses will pay to not only be seen in this portion of the search results but also when someone clicks. The focus of this chapter, however, is on the rest of the results — the ones that are not paid advertisements — referred to as "organic."

Google Local Map Results: AKA 'Snack Pack'

Next, under the two advertisements (often four ads appear at the top in competitive markets), we have the list of the Google Map results. This section of the search results is often called the "Snack Pack" by Local SEO marketers.

Several years ago, Google had seven map results, and then then five... and now just three, and in some cases only two... which is why it's been dubbed a "snack." If you are a local business, you want to be found here! These are "Google My Business" listings. (Google My Business[2] is a free and easy-to-use tool for businesses, brands, artists, and organizations to manage their online presence across Google, including Search and Maps.)

Organic Website Results

Below the Snack Pack is a list of web pages. This is another area of the search results where you will want to focus on ranking, in addition to the Snack Pack.

The Golden Trifecta

I've talked with many business owners — and have seen this first hand with my own clients — who attest that having your business appear in the advertisements, Snack Pack, and organic website results, can produce a high volume of leads, calls, and customers. I have also read studies that show people often click on the organic website result when a paid advertisement appears. I strongly recommend that you strive to be in all three areas, and include PPC as part of your marketing plan.

Mobile Search Results from a Browser

Below is a series of screenshots for the search results for the same query — "cosmetic dentists

denver co" — performed from my iPhone using a
Google Chrome browser.

Below is the first screenshot. Notice how it is
entirely full of ads? You don't even see the Snack
Pack or the organic website results!

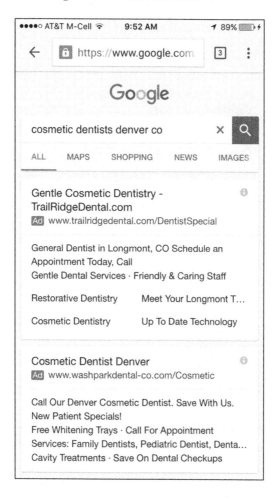

Next is a screenshot after I scroll down past the two advertisements. You see two more ads, and then the Snack Pack, with three listings.

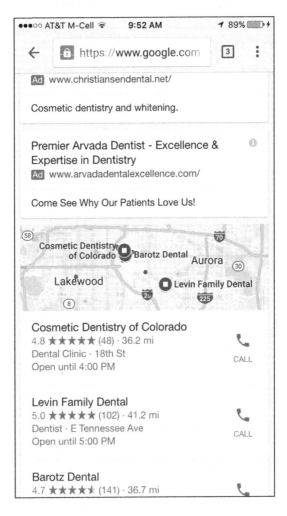

A third screenshot, shown below, is after I scroll past the local pack. The first two results are local businesses, then a Yelp page listing cosmetic dentists, and then a local business.

●●●○○ AT&T M-Cell 🗢   9:53 AM   🢁 89% 🔋⚡

Down Town Denverdentist: Home
www.downtowndenverdentist.com

Mobile-friendly - 3 days ago - Dr. Radz and the Cosmetic Dentistry of Colorado team welcome you to Denver's best in dental and ...

Veneers & Cosmetic Dentistry | Dental Implants & Crowns - Denver
www.levinfamilydental.com

Mobile-friendly - Levin Family Dental is Denver's top dentist's office providing cosmetic dentistry, dental implants, veneers & more.
Contact · Meet our Team · Jennifer L. Derse DDS

Cosmetic Dentistry of Colorado - Cosmetic Dentists - Northwest - Denver, CO ... - Yelp
Yelp › ... › Dentists › Cosmetic Dentists

★★★★⯪ Rating: 4.5 - 7 reviews
Mobile-friendly - (303) 298-1414 · Cosmetic Dentists, General Dentistry ... Cosmetic Dentistry of Colorado - Denver, CO, United States.

Cosmetic Dentist | Barotz Dental | Teeth Whitening Denver
www.barotzdental.com › cosmetic-dentist...

Mobile Search Results from Siri

Next, I asked my iPhone, using voice search with Siri, for "Cosmetic Dentists Denver CO." Here's what it pulled up.

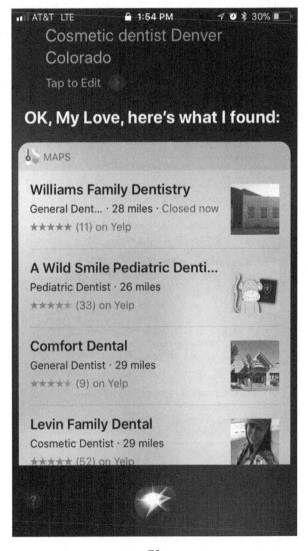

Notice how these are all Apple Maps results showing Yelp reviews? Also, notice how they're very different from the businesses listed in the Snack Pack? At the time of this writing, iPhone's Siri search (as well as Apple Maps results for businesses) is influenced largely by Yelp.

A Quick Rundown on Local Search Ranking Factors

While there are a lot of factors involved in getting your business found in search engines for your desired keywords, here's a summary of what you need to know to have a basic understanding of Local SEO.

Website On-page SEO

First, there's on-page SEO, which refers to the SEO settings on the pages of your website. This includes things like using keywords in your Page Title Tags, Meta Descriptions, the text on your web pages, Schema, and other settings that help search engines understand what your site is about.

<u>On-page SEO represents about *only* 14% of your positioning in the Local Pack (map results) and 24% of your ranking in the organic results (webpage links beneath the maps)</u>, according to the Moz 2017 Local Search Survey.[3] In other words, **75-85% of getting found in local searches is NOT just adding keywords to your website,**

which is contrary to what most business owners assume.

Many businesses also falsely assume that their site has been optimized because they install an SEO plugin or because their website comes with the *option* to customize SEO settings. But, really, there's a lot more to be done than just launching a site with a plugin. You need to research the words and content and add them according to Google's *current* guidelines — a constantly moving target.

Local Directories, Apps, and NAP

Next, there are local directories, maps, and apps such as Google My Business, Google Maps, Apple Maps, Yelp, Facebook, Foursquare, and others. These directories contain listing data like your business name, address, and phone number — referred to as NAP in the SEO industry. Having complete profiles and consistent NAP information across the web is extremely important.

Reviews

Review sites such as Yelp and Google My Business are increasingly important, especially on mobile search. Not only are reviews a ranking factor, but they also have a huge influence on purchasing decisions.

Behavioral Signals

Clicks to call from your Google listing, directions, click through rate (the amount of people who actually click onto your site after seeing it in the search results), time spent on site, and other behaviors influence search engine positioning.

Links

Last, but most certainly not least, the number and quality of links pointing to your site from other websites is a critical part of Local SEO and is, by far, the area where most businesses struggle. Using links as part of their ranking algorithm was part of PageRank, Google's patented algorithm — a key differentiator from search engines like Yahoo. If you're a nerd, you could read about it here: www.ilpubs.stanford.edu:8090/422/1/1999-66.pdf.

Claim and Optimize Your
Google My Business Listing

Being listed with your correct information in Google My Business (GMB) is critical for local businesses to get found in Google Search, Maps, and Google Plus. While there are several external factors that influence the visibility of your GMB Listing — such as the content on your website and inbound links, which we'll explain in the other sections of the book — the information that you list in the Google My Business listing is highly important.

Be found by customers across Google

Think of Your Google
My Business Listing like a Mini Website

For mobile consumers on the go, the information on your Google My Business listing may be the only information they need to see in order to make a decision about whether they'll choose you over a competitor. Treat your GMB listing like a mini website and be sure to complete it with store hours, a link to your website, correct phone number and address, and perhaps most importantly, **professional photos that make your business look attractive.**

Your Google My Business listing is a central part of your online presence. Google will show this to your (future) customers, and it's vital that the information listed here be accurate.

Google doesn't want to disappoint its users, or else they'll head over to Bing or Yahoo. Having correct and consistent information here is imperative!

Five Tips for Optimizing Your Google My Business Listing

1. Claim and Verify Your Listing at Google.com/business/

Make sure that you have accurate Name, Address, and Phone Number. You will need to follow a verification process to receive a postcard in the mail to prove to Google that you actually exist where you say you do.

2. Update Your Store Hours + Special Hours

Having current store hours is critical to get found in search queries like "open now near me", and so on, so make sure your hours are up to date. If you have special holiday hours when you're open late or closed, be sure to update those as well. Check out ramblinjackson.com/holidayguide/ for info on how to do that.

3. Showcase Your Business with Photos

Photos are a HUGE opportunity! Uploading photos regularly can help you get found ahead of your competition. More importantly, people might not look past your Google My Business listing and into your website if you have poor photos.

Here are some of the categories for photos you can have:

- Interior
- Exterior
- Team
- At work
- Identity

Potential employees will likely Google them. Make your company look like a great place to work with current, engaging photos.

In the front range of Colorado, there are over 200 marketing companies offering services similar to my company. But because we practice what we preach, we get 889% more views of our photos than our competitors — according to our Google My Business insights. Imagine if you updated your photos regularly!

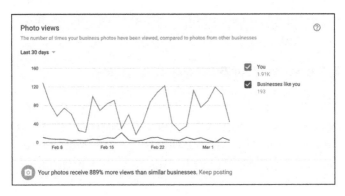

4. Select Relevant Categories

Select as many categories that are as relevant to
your business as possible. A great tool for searching
out the different categories is the Moz Category
tool: www.moz.com/local/categories

5. Update Google Posts Regularly

In the summer of 2017, Google released a feature
called Google Posts, which is kind of similar to a
post made from a Facebook Page. A post shows up
in the Search results underneath your Google My
Business listing. It can be a photo that also has a
link to a blog post, event, or other page on your
website. I have seen an increase in my own ranking
and have read several studies from other SEO
professionals that using Google post has a mild
impact on your rankings in Google+. I recommend
using it.

Watch a video interview with the
office manager of an arborist who
increased sales 30% in one year of
implementing Local SEO and a new website
at ramblinjackson.com/arborist/

Here's an example of how Google Post looks under your Google My Business listing:

On Desktop:

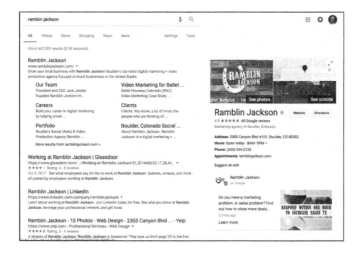

On Mobile:

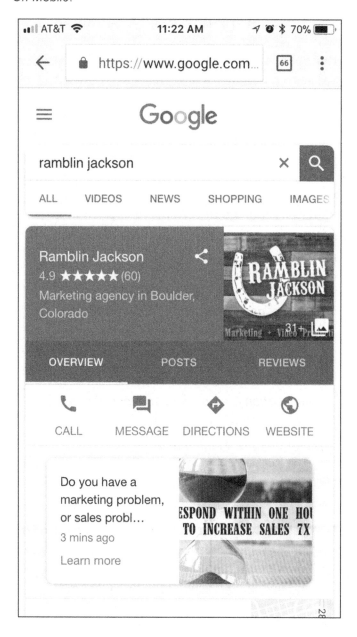

Google Confirms How
Local Rankings Are Determined

After years of being relatively vague about how local search actually works, Google FINALLY confirmed what Ramblin Jackson and the Local SEO community has been saying for years: Inbound links, on-page SEO, and positive reviews help your rankings in local results.

Here's what was published on a Google My Business help page in the spring of 2016 in a section called "How Google determines local ranking":[4]

> *"Local results are based primarily on relevance, distance, and prominence. These factors are combined to help find the best match for your search. For example, Google algorithms might decide that a business that's farther away from your location is more likely to have what you're looking for than a business that's closer, and therefore rank it higher in local results."*

Relevance

Relevance refers to how well a local listing matches what someone is searching for. Adding complete and detailed business information can help Google better understand your business and match your listing to relevant searches.

Distance

Just like it sounds — how far is each potential search result from the location term used in a search? If a user doesn't specify a location in their search, Google will calculate distance based on what's known about their location.

Prominence

Prominence refers to how well-known a business is. Some places are more prominent in the offline world, and search results try to reflect this in local ranking. For example, famous museums, landmark hotels, or well-known store brands that are familiar to many people are also likely to be prominent in local search results.

Prominence is also based on information that Google has about a business from across the web (such as links, articles, and directories). Google review count and score are factored into local search ranking: more reviews and positive ratings will probably improve a business's local ranking. Your position in web results is also a factor, so SEO best practices also apply to local search optimization.

There's no way to request or pay for a better local ranking on Google. We do our best to keep the details of the search algorithm confidential to make the ranking system as fair as possible for everyone. (See a short video about this at bit.ly/FRR214.)

While you cannot control the distance of your potential customers from your business, you can absolutely influence how Google perceives the relevance of your website and online listings as well as the prominence. And you can certainly influence the accuracy of the information online that will help people near your business find you more easily.

There are many individual aspects of Local SEO that impact rankings, which I'll touch on later in this chapter. Now that you have a basic understanding of Local SEO and what the search engine results look like for local search queries, let's talk about how you can get your business found there.

Variety of Mobile Device Search Options Increasing

It's important to understand *how* your customers are searching for you, and it's vital that you know that they will likely interact with your brand on a variety of devices — mobile, tablet, and/or desktop computers — before choosing to do business with you.

We all know that mobile searches are growing. But *how*? How people search is changing, which affects what you need to do to be found.

In addition to the variety of different devices, there are a range of ways to search from mobile:

1. **Through a browser** (Google Chrome, Firefox, Safari, etc.) and then a variety of different search engines (i.e. Google, Bing, Yahoo, Duck Duck Go, etc.);

2. **Through voice search with a personal assistant** like Siri or Android voice searches with OK Google or Google Voice;

3. **Through apps** such as Google Maps, Apple Maps, Yelp, Foursquare, Facebook, and more.

To get found in the many ways people search, local businesses must optimize their online presence in ways beyond just traditional on-page SEO and major directories.

Consumers are three times more likely to use voice search for a local query, according to Search Engine Watch.[5]

That means that your customers are likely asking browsers, apps, or voice assistants such as Siri, Cortana, or OK Google, for things like "best chinese restaurant near me open now." There has been a

2.1X increase in mobile searches for "stores open now" or "food open now" in the past year.[6]

Customers Are Searching "Near Me," "Open Now," "Best," "Gluten-Free"

The queries people search are becoming increasingly longer, more specific, and focused on providing results showing a business closest to the person's physical location (or, rather, a business nearest the device from which they're searching).

Below is a graph of the search trends for the query, "Best chinese restaurants near me," according to Google Trends.

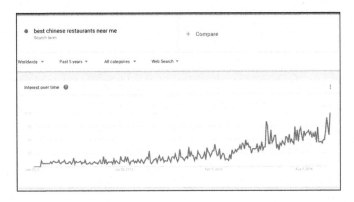

As you can see, this query has nearly tripled — just in the last two years.

Here's another less specific search trend for "Restaurants near me" where the trend is even clearer.

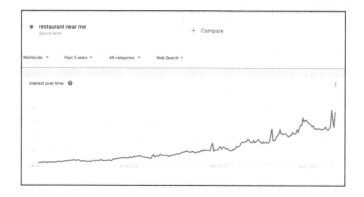

More and more, consumers can find whatever they're thinking about, open now, and even better — the *best* business *nearest their device* that's *open now* offering whatever they want.

This isn't just happening for restaurants. I see these trends across many industries, including fitness, health and wellness, dental, automotive, and more.

Get Found in Directories with Consistent Name, Address, Phone (NAP) Citations

Because people are searching more and more "near me," the accuracy and consistency of the data on the internet regarding the location of your business has never been more important. For search engines, apps, and voice assistants to *trust that you are where you say you are* enough to show your business as a result, you need to have consistent citations online.

What are citations?

A citation is an online mention of your Business Name, Address, and Phone Number. This is also referred to as NAP in the marketing industry. What's most important is that your information is listed *consistently* everywhere online.

Common Issues with NAP Citations

Think about this: If you were a map, and you made your living when people used you to get around, how long would you stay in business if people who used your map got lost as a result of your bad directions? Not very long. That's why having *consistent* information in all of your citations is so critical. If Google Maps isn't 100% certain that you are where you say you are, that you're open and in business, why would they risk showing someone your business when they're searching for "restaurants near me open now?"

Unfortunately, it's all too common that businesses have inconsistent information online that interferes with their rankings in local searches. Worse, they typically don't know — and wonder for ages — why they're not showing up in search results like they want to.

Here's how NAP citations can become inconsistent:

1. **Human error.** An intern, employee, or inattentive business owner will create

online listings and accidentally add inconsistent information to them (i.e., for the business name field, Yelp will say "Bob's Taco Shop," Facebook will say "Bob's Tacos," Google Maps will say "Bob's Tacos Shop, Inc.," and so on. You get the idea. The same opportunity for error happens with the address field and the phone number field.

2. **Changing business name or address.** Another common reason that citations become inconsistent is that a business will move or alter its business name in a rebranding and only update *some* of the directories.

3. **Phone company sells an old phone number to a new business.** One time, a used car lot wasn't even ranking when they searched "used cars near me" from their own lot. I investigated their phone number and discovered that the phone number had previously belonged to another business that was now closed. The old business had hundreds of citations with their phone number, creating a huge mess for the used car lot.

Six months after hiring me to fix this issue, that auto dealer wrote that our helped saved them from going out of business — that's what's at stake with your NAP.

How Tony P Lost 30% in Revenue from NAP Inconsistencies

You might be bored. You might think this is still a bunch of SEO jargon B.S. you don't want to deal with. And that's fine. But if it cost you 30% in revenue, you might feel differently. And a 30% loss is what happened to Tony Pasquini, pizza shop owner in Denver.

I grew up in Chicagoland and love Chicago-style deep dish pizza. Not long ago, while preparing for a presentation on SEO at HubSpot's INBOUND Conference in Boston, the world's largest digital marketing conference, I did a search for "pizza Denver." I thought, "I'm going to pick somebody who's on the last page of Google for this terms and figure out what did they do wrong, how they are screwing this up so badly." There are over 20 pages of search results for businesses who offer pizza in Denver. I went to the very last page and I found this place, Tony P's.

It turns out Tony's SEO is a mess. I googled his business name and just look at all the variations I found of his business name right on the first page.

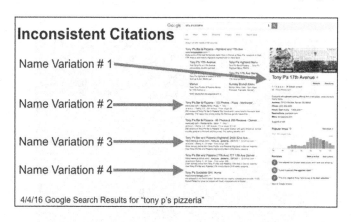

1. There's "Tony P's 17th Avenue";

2. Then there's "Tony P's Bar & Pizzeria" with the ampersand;

3. Then there's "Tony P's Bar and Pizzeria (Highland)" with the word "pizzeria" spelled out with highland and parentheses;

4. And then there's "Tony P's Bar and Pizzeria (17th Ave.)."

I looked up Tony's phone number and gave him a call. I asked, "Hey Tony, do you know your SEO is terrible?" His answer: "Dude, I get calls like this everyday." I offered to drop by his restaurant, have some pizza, and talk SEO. "Alright, fine," he said.

Tony had to step away from our conversation for a moment and I took the opportunity to ask Siri for "pizza near me." Here's a screenshot of the search results.

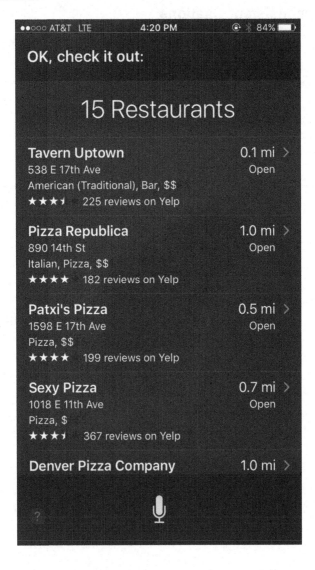

I was in the restaurant holding a piece of pizza in my hand. Pizza couldn't possibly be more near me! But Tony's is not even listed there. So I hopped on his WiFi network on my computer and googled his business name. It showed the place across town.

I'm at the 17th avenue location, but it showed his business all the way across town. I searched "pizza near me" again on my computer and he was still nowhere to be found. I thought, **how much money does this guy pay to rent that building, to be there, to not be found by people searching for "pizza near me?"**

There's a concert venue just a couple blocks away. It's Colorado... There are a lot of people at concerts looking for pizza.

When I asked Tony how this happened, he said, "We had a conglomerate of six restaurants called Pasquini's, which we rebranded to Tony P's. We did everything we could to let our customers know that we are Tony P's now and that we are here. But when we changed our name, our business went down 30% at some locations. That made it difficult to not only reach our customer base but also to pay our bills."

Nap consistency may sound like a bunch of business jargon until it costs you 30% in sales. That's what's at stake here.

How to Find NAP Inconsistencies

One tool you can use to see how consistent your online citations are is Moz Local, a paid service you can use to get submitted to a lot of different directories. I use it as part of my local SEO process, and think it's generally good. Moz Local also has a free search tool where you can type in your business name and your ZIP Code and it will show you what citations are out there.

In addition to using a software like Moz, I recommend that you Google your phone number in the following format: (123) 123-1234. When you search a phone number in Google using that format, it will pull up nearly every listing (that's indexed by Google) containing your phone number.

Do a search for that with a combination of any old addresses and/or business names you have and look at the results to find the inconsistencies. This is how I found out that my used car lot client's phone number actually belonged to another business, something that not even Moz Local would have observed.

How to Attract Your Perfect Client with Keyword Research

One of the most important parts of Local SEO is choosing keywords that will actually drive customers towards your business. You'll use your keywords in your website text, descriptions on social networks and directories, and in your site's SEO settings. Before you edit the content on your website and listings, however, do some research to choose the best keyword opportunities.

> Keyword research is the process of finding out what phrases your potential customers are searching to find businesses like yours. Without doing keyword research, you're just guessing at what people are searching.

An effective keyword research campaign will involve using a research tool like Google Adwords Keyword Planner[7] to see what kind of search volume is behind your ideas for potential keywords, some competitive analysis of what businesses and website are ranking for your desired keywords, and strategic thinking about the *intent* of the person making the searches.

In particular, you want to find keywords that have the intent behind them of someone looking to do business with someone exactly like you and keywords that have a realistic level of competition.

To get quality leads online, you need to get found for the right keywords. Not all are created equally. A lot of people will rush through this, mistakenly trusting someone outside of their business (like an SEO company) to just run with it (without giving them enough insight into the business), or they assume that they know what other people would be searching because they've been doing this for 20 years. Many business owners never look at the data or think critically about its implications on how their business will be found online and by whom.

Consider this example:

Chiropractors dream about chiropractic. They went to school for chiropractic. They have books about chiropractic in their office. They geek out about chiropractic every day when they look at their chiropractic spine charts on the wall. And they assume that everyone else is thinking about "chiropractic" and assume that "chiropractic" is their keyword of choice.

But let's take a quick peek at some keyword research about chiropractic. (I got the following data using Moz's Keyword Explorer tool.[8]) In the left column, we see the keyword and, in the right, the volume of searches on a monthly basis. Clearly, more people are searching for "chiropractor" than "chiropractic." Thus, it would be a better keyword.

☐	Keyword ↓↑	Volume ↓
☐	**chiropractor denver** United States - en-US	851-1.7k
☐	**chiropractic denver** United States - en-US	51-100

I once did SEO for a brilliant dentist who had an eco-friendly dental office. He hired me because no one could find him on Google and he didn't have enough new patients. He was extremely embarrassed to learn that he didn't even have the word "dentist" on his website homepage before I edited it! Instead, his content was really geeky and technical and focused on "dentistry" without using any keyword research and without describing any benefit to his potential patients.

It's not uncommon for business owners, especially ones with technical expertise such as dentists or architects, to write technical-sounding copy that excludes keywords and language that would resonate with the end customers. I strongly recommend having an SEO copy editor review your website content after it's written to make sure that it has the right keywords and reads well.

The Criteria of a Profitable Local SEO Keyword

Selecting keywords is as much art as science. While we can use data from keyword tools like Google Adwords Keyword Planner as part of the process, we can't rely on the numbers alone without considering the subjective context of what the words actually mean and what people want when they search them. Every small business owner, or at least a marketing manager or salesperson who intimately understands the business's customers and what motivates them to buy, should be involved in the keyword selection process.

SEO Tip: Never let a third party pick your keywords without someone from your business providing the strategic sales insight. I'll describe below.

A good local SEO keyword will have:

- Strong monthly search volume;

- Relevance to your product or service;

- High business value; Realistic competition;

- Local Pack or local business results when searched without a geographic modifier;

- Most importantly, the **intent to hire a local human or go to a local store.**

Unless you're running an ecommerce site (in which case this book isn't meant for you), the keyword you select must have the intent of someone looking for a local brick-and-mortar business versus someone searching for a product or service they can purchase online.

To help you understand what I mean by selecting a keyword that has the intent of finding a local business, I'd like to show you an example of some keyword research and I want you to pretend for a minute that you're the owner of a local spa.

You own a spa that offers massages, skin care services, and, maybe, acupuncture. You're a located in a busy metropolitan area with a large population. We've done some keyword research for you, and we've set the filter in the Google AdWords tool to your city, which, in this case, happens to be Denver. The research shows that there are 90 searches a month for "skin care products" from Denver and, also, 50 searches a month for "facials Denver."

At my presentation at INBOUND, I presented this keyword research and posed this question to the audience: "Which one is better keyword for your spa, 'skin care products' or 'facials denver?'"

"I think most women are looking for skin care products," said a woman in response. "Even if you're going to get your hair done, they have it, you go to a massage place you have it done, you go get your hair done. I think a lot of people search for that."

When I did a quick poll of the audience, well more than half thought that "skin care products" was a better result than "facials denver," and several people said they thought so because there were more searches for "skin care products."

Let's take a look at the search results when we type those phrases in Google. This is a missing step that a lot of people don't do. Many people just look at the search volume and say, "This one has more," and they don't do this next step of doing a search and analyzing the existing results.

Here are the search result for "skin care products":

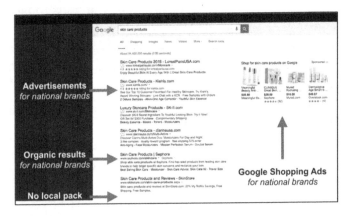

At the top, we have advertisements from Google AdWords for national brands like L'Oreal and Kiehl's. We also have Google Shopping ads; people that are paying Google to be in Google Shopping with advertisements from brands like Sephora and Overstock — big brands with big budgets. Then, in the organic results, we see, again, *national* brands. There's no local Snack Pack at all. Google knows from the location of my device that I'm in Denver. It knows where I am, and all I'm seeing are these big national companies with big budgets that I can never compete with.

Now, let's look at the search results for "facials Denver":

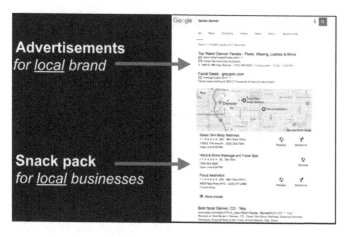

At the top, one of the key distinctions here is we see advertisements again, but we see them for a *local* business. Below it we see the Snack Pack. We see local businesses with map results in the city where I was searching.

Now that you have looked at the search results, which one do you think would be a better choice, "skin care products" or "facials Denver?" If you selected "facials Denver" after taking a closer look, like the audience at the INBOUND did, you're on the right track!

Keyword Research Tip: Don't get too focused on the monthly search volume numbers alone.

Don't let your AdWords guy tell you that, "This is an organic keyword," if they don't do organic SEO. They're two different things; advertising and organic SEO are related, but they're two different algorithms. One is paying for advertising; one is organic. The Google Adwords Keyword Planner is a great tool, but you can't use it alone. Always, always, always do the search and make sure that you choose a result where you can see yourself.

Target keywords that have the intent of somebody hiring a *local* business and not somebody that's looking to just buy something online. Skin care products is something I can buy online, and I'm just going to price shop. I'm going to find the cheapest price and order it online, and a small local business likely can't compete with that in ecommerce.

You need to get into your client's head.

- What would your perfect client actually search?

- What problem do you solve for them?

- What problem do you solve for them?

- What do people ask on the phone? "Hey, do you guys do facials in Denver? Okay. Good."

Write down commonly asked questions. What questions are people emailing you? What are people commenting on Facebook? They're probably googling those things too, and that can be ideal content for your website and blog.

How to Become a Big Fish in a Small Pond

I love fishing. There's an endless sea of parallels between fishing and business, and there's one that's really relevant to local SEO.

One morning before work, I went fishing with one of my employees at the Boulder Reservoir — the largest body of water in Boulder (excluding the many rivers that run through).

When we arrived, it was dried up and had a very low water level. This picture was taken from the middle of the reservoir. It was almost completely dried up! There were tons of fishermen there but no sign of fish. We just assumed, "Oh, the biggest lake in Boulder, it must have the best fishing, right?"

It was a crisp spring Colorado morning and the geese they were a-honking. Since the Boulder Reservoir was all dried up, we ventured to a small pond — a secret pond that Steve from McGuckin Hardware told us about. After hours of tranquility and no bites... we saw a monster fish lurk from the water. It may have tried to eat a duck on the water. It was so "ginormous" it could hardly get its whole body out of the water and caused a big ruckus as it splashed back. I cast a Senko Texas Rig in his direction, and soon reeled in this enormous large-mouth bass!

That was exhilarating! (You can watch a video of me catching this bass and see some photos at www.ramblinjackson.com/bigfishsmallpond/.)

What does this have to do with SEO? **As a local business, you can be a big fish in a small pond when it comes to your keywords.** Of course, you should always go for the short tail phrases like "facials Denver," "tires Chicago," or whatever is most relevant and, likely, most competitive in your industry.

A short-tail phrase is just a search phrase containing fewer keywords, and they tend to have higher search volume and also higher competitive. But you also want to find long-tail phrases that have less competition. For example, "Auto repair cincinnati" would be an example of a short-tail phrase and "Subaru Outback repair shops cincinnati" would be an example of a long-tail phrase.

What are the long tail niche products or services that you offer for that specific perfect customer that you're targeting, and what would they search that your competition isn't trying to rank for?

A key component of a perfect customer is their ability and willingness to pay. Can your clients afford what you do? Which are best at that? Which can definitely afford what you do? Which ones can you charge the most to? What would they search?

How One Webpage Created Over $200,000 for a Pilates Studio

Let's use a real-life example of a Pilates studio for this long-tail keyword phrase idea.

My digital marketing agency, Ramblin Jackson, works with Firehaus Pilates, a Pilates studio in Denver that helps people overcome pain from sports and other injuries.

Denver is an extremely competitive market when it comes to Pilates because there are over forty studios in the area. When developing their keyword strategy, we dug deep into Firehaus Pilates' various types of customers and learned the product they *really* sell is pain relief. They help people who are in pain get physical rehabilitation through Pilates.

We thought, who's in pain and has money to spend that also has the time and willingness to invest in exercise and show up to class? The answer? Senior women over age 60.

Another benefit of this market is that the customer has kids my age who are searching for things for her to do to relieve this pain. Grandma and her kids are googling this kind of thing, and we know that based on the keyword research.

We looked at the numbers. There are tons of searches a month. There aren't nearly as many as there are for the short tail phrase, "Pilates Denver," but after doing some analysis of the search results, there's also far fewer people fishing for these long tail keywords, which creates a great opportunity for Firehaus to not only rank quickly on the first page of Google but also, more importantly, capture a profitable segment of the market.

After we selected that keyword phrase "pilates for seniors denver," we created a page on Firehaus' website that speaks to the pains and challenges the senior market faces, with copy tailored to how Firehaus Pilates can help them, photos of real seniors in the studio, and a video featuring interviews of the women in the class and how Pilates has helped them. The page ranks very highly in Google, and when someone looking for pilates classes for seniors in Denver finds it, they know that they're in the right place and that Firehaus understands how to help.

Firehaus Pilates' owner, Rachel Algra, sent me this picture. Two of the three women pictured found her on Google, searching Pilates for Denver. The third is a friend that one brought along.

What's your niche market, and what are they searching?

In your business, what is the particular niche market that you serve? What's the long-tail keyword phrase you can target that your competitors maybe aren't, where you can rank really quickly and get a bunch of leads?

The main point to remember is to choose keywords that a profitable niche market would search. Become a big fish in a small pond and remember that each page of your website is an opportunity for SEO. Google doesn't rank websites, Google ranks web pages.

Key Takeaways From How To Get Found By Your Perfect Customers With Local SEO - Part 1

- Local SEO is the process of helping a local business get found online in the websites, directories, and search engines commonly used by consumers who are searching for a local business.

- To get found, you need to do ALL the aspects of Local SEO.

- 75-85% of getting found in local searches is NOT just adding keywords to your website, which is contrary to what most business owners assume.

- Make sure your NAP (Name, Address, and Phone Number) is consistent online.

- Target keywords that have the *intent* of someone looking for a *local* business (vs. an online purchase).

- Hustle for reviews! Get reviews on Google, Facebook, Yelp, and wherever else is relevant to your industry.

6

How to Get Found by Your Perfect Customers with Local SEO Part 2

"God is in the details."

- Ludwig Mies van der Rohe

Now that you have a basic understanding of how local SEO works plus how to select your target keywords, it's time to roll up your internet sleeves and get to work to help people find you!

In this part, we'll go into greater detail on how to implement SEO, how to optimize the content on your website, how to write schema on your site, and how to outrank your competition with link building and other advanced tactics. You'll learn how to take a close look at search results and break down what the businesses on the first page are doing to get found.

Get Found in Search Results with On-Page SEO

Now that you've identified the keywords phrases for which you want your business to get found, it's time to help search engines know that your website is relevant to those keyword phrases through on-page SEO. In this section, you'll learn how to write website text using your keywords and which website settings you need to adjust.

On-Page SEO is the process of updating the metadata and content of a website so search engines properly associate it with the desired keyword phrases. It is called "on-page SEO" because the work is being done directly *on* the web pages. There is also "off-page SEO" — the work that needs to be done externally from your website, such as link building, reviews, citation building, and so on.

Google Ranks Web Pages Not Websites

When developing your on-page SEO strategy, it's important to remember that Google ranks individual web pages, not websites, in its search results. Each page of your website is an opportunity to rank in Google for a specific search phrase.

Let's take a look at the search results for "wheel alignment madison WI":

For reference, I searched this from a MacBook Air using Google Chrome as my browser on 12/27/17.

Best Wheel alignment in Madison, WI - Yelp
https://www.yelp.com/search?find_desc=wheel+alignment&find...Madison%2C+WI ▾
Reviews on **Wheel alignment** in **Madison, WI** - Hansen's Auto, CV Pros, West Town Monona Tire,
Accurate Alignment Service, Jenks Service Center, Discount Tire Store · **Madison, WI**, Reece's Auto &
Restorati, Midas, Firestone Complete Auto Care, Meineke...

Auto Wheel Alignment | Madison, WI Firestone Complete Auto Care
https://local.firestonecompleteautocare.com › Wisconsin › Madison ▾
Choose Us For **Wheel Alignment** in **Madison**. is your **car's** fuel economy not what it used to be? It might
be time for a **wheel alignment**. Misalignment problems often come from everyday occurrences like
driving over potholes, but can also arise after major incidents like a collision.

Four-Wheel Alignment Monona, WI | Broadway Tire And Auto
https://www.broadwaytireauto.com/auto.../wheel-alignment/four-wheel-alignment.asp... ▾
Wheels can become misaligned during a **car** crash or by simply hitting road obstructions, like potholes
or curbs. There are several signs that will alert you to an impending four-**wheel alignment** service. A
vehicle pulling strongly to one side is in need of **alignment**. Another sign is uneven or abnormal tire wear.

Best 30 Cheap Auto Alignment in Madison, WI with Reviews - YP.com
https://www.yellowpages.com/madison-wi/cheap-auto-alignment ▾
469 results · Specialized cheap auto **alignment** in **Madison, WI**. Access BBB ratings, makes serviced,
certifications, and more · THE REAL YELLOW PAGES®

Best 30 Wheel Alignment Prices in Madison, WI with Reviews - YP.com
https://www.yellowpages.com/madison-wi/wheel-alignment-prices ▾
78 results · **Wheel Alignment** Prices in Madison on YP.com. See reviews, photos, directions, phone
numbers and more for the best Wheels-Aligning & Balancing in **Madison, WI**.

Wheel Alignment near Madison, WI | Car Alignment near me
www.clausenautomotive.com/wheel-alignment-madison-wi ▾
★★★★★ Rating: 5 - 68 reviews · Price range: $$$
Get Proper **Wheel Alignment** & Balancing by Clausen Automotive experts. Visit us at 2118 S. Stoughton
Rd., **Madison, WI**, 53716. Call 608-221-8321.

Wheel Alignment Madison, WI | Chet's Car Care
www.chetscarcare.com/auto-repairs/wheel-alignment.aspx ▾
Stop your vehicle pulling to the left or right and protect against unusual tire wear with a **wheel alignment**
from Chet's Car Care. Call our team today!

Two-Wheel Alignment Madison, WI | Chet's Car Care
www.chetscarcare.com/auto-repairs/wheel-alignment/two-wheel-alignment.aspx ▾
Need a 2 **wheel alignment**? Schedule your next service with Chet's Car Care to keep your tires pointing
correctly. We serve **Madison, WI**, Cottage Grove, WI, Sun Prairie, WI.

Wheel Alignment in Madison, WI | Capitol Tire And Service
https://captire.net/wheel-alignments-madison-wi ▾
Wheel Alignment is done at the time brand-new tires are set up, and can easily be checked with your
regular tire rotation. Capitol Tire And Service offers quality affordable **Madison, WI** auto repair services.
What it does: Wheels must be lined up correctly to keep suitable control of your car. Wheels that are out
of position ...

Auto Repair & Service | CVPro Axle Service | Madison WI
www.cvpros.com/ ▾
CV Pros Axle Service provide many auto repairs including **Wheel** bearings, brakes, shocks, struts,
suspensions, chassis/steering parts, & **wheel** alignments.

Wheel Alignment - Madison
[Ad] www.capitoltire.biz/ ▾
Do You Need **Wheel Alignment**? Call Now Or Come In To Get Started.
Contact Us · Brake & Wheel Services

At the top of the results, we see Google Adwords advertisements for Haglin Auto, Auroras Best Auto Repair, Goodyear Auto Service, and Sears Auto Center.

Then, in the Snack Pack, we see three Google My Business listings for Clausen Automotive, Capitol Tire and Service, and CV Pros. *Notice those little review snippets with the little blue person icon next to it? That wasn't there when I started writing this book! This looks to me like Google is incorporating reviews more and more into its algorithm for local.*

Beneath the Snack Pack, there are ten organic webpage results, which I have outlined below. I have also bolded the words from my search query: wheel, alignment, Madison, and WI in the URLS to illustrate a point about using keywords in your URLs (which I will explain later in this chapter.)

Here are the URLs of the web pages that rank on the first page of Google beneath the Snack Pack for "wheel alignment madison WI":

1. www.yelp.com/search?find_desc=wheel+alignment&find...madison%2C+WI

2. www.local.firestonecompleteautocare.com/wisconsin/madison/alignment/

3. www.broadwaytireauto.com/auto-repairs/wheel-alignment/four-wheel-alignment.aspx

4. www.yellowpages.com/madison-wi/cheap-auto-alignment

5. www.yellowpages.com/madison-wi/wheel-alignment-prices

6. www.clausenautomotive.com/wheel-alignment-madison-wi

7. www.chetscarcare.com/auto-repairs/wheel-alignment.aspx

8. www.chetscarcare.com/auto-repairs/wheel-alignment/two-wheel-alignment.aspx

9. www.captire.net/wheel-alignments-madison-wi

10. www.cvpros.com/

Observations about
Organic Website Results

Web Pages vs. Websites

With the exception of CV Pros, whose homepage, cvpros.com, ranks in the number 10 position, the remaining results are *individual pages* on those *websites specific to wheel alignment* and/or *Madison, WI* instead of just their homepage.

Google ranks web *pages* not websites.

Many business owners think "my site is optimized" — but they don't know if they have individual *pages* going for each query.

At the very bottom of the page, beneath the organic webpage results, there are two Google Adwords advertisements for Hansen's Auto Service Center and the Wrench Greeley.

Review Schema

See those stars under Clausen Automotive? Dang! That looks great. Nice work, Clausen! They're using review schema, which we'll discuss later in the chapter.

Wheel Alignment near Madison, WI | Car Alignment near me
www.clausenautomotive.com/wheel-alignment-madison-wi ▾
★ ★ ★ ★ ★ Rating: 5 - 68 reviews - Price range: $$$
Get Proper **Wheel Alignment** & Balancing by Clausen Automotive experts. Visit us at 2118 S. Stoughton
Rd., **Madison**, WI, 53716. Call 608-221-8321.

How to Develop Your On-Page
SEO Strategy Page-by-Page

When you're creating your on-page SEO strategy,
take it service by service and page by page.

When you have grouped your keyword research
into keyword categories (like I suggested in the
section about keyword research), that can be a
great way to determine what and how many pages
you should have. The best way to do this is to think
like your potential customer — what would be most
helpful for them to find when they are a searching?

Which would be more helpful to them: a generic
page of vague content with sparse information
about your "services" or a page with content
customized to the person that answers a specific
need or challenge they have and that positions your
business as the best resource?

Here are a few ideas for how you could brainstorm
what individual pages you might need:

A Page per Product or Service

For example, a dentist could have a page for
cosmetic dentistry, a page for family dentistry, a
page for crowns, and so on.

A Page per Event

A business coach or professional consultant who regularly conducts webinars, workshops, or events for different audiences and/or locations could have a page for your Chicago workshops in addition to the "Events" page.

A Page per Dentist, Doctor, or Lawyer

A dental office, doctor's office, law firm, or business with multiple partners or practitioners could have an individual bio page for each person and optimize it for their specialty keyword.

For example, you could have a bio page for Dr. Tom Jones optimized for "cosmetic dentist" and Dr. Jane Sanchez's bio page could be optimized for "sedation dentist" if that was her specialty.

A Page per Location and/or Geographic Service Area

A business with multiple physical brick and mortar locations or a service area business such as a plumber or window replacement company could create individual pages for each geographic market. These are called *Local Landing Pages*.

An excellent example of a business that does this well is CorePower Yoga, a yoga studio franchise with more than 150 locations located in major cities and suburbs throughout the United States.

If you search for "yoga studios" in any city that has a CorePower Yoga studio, chances are you'll find them ranking very highly in search results. This is due, in part, to their website being extremely well-organized in a way that the URL structure includes "yoga studios" "state" and "city."

Each location page has information helpful to a potential yogi customer: schedule information, bios and photos of the instructors, map/location/parking/contact details, and an option to sign up for that location's email newsletter, to get relevant updates.

Here's a screenshot of search results for "yoga studios arlington heights IL."

Notice how CorePower is in the local pack (snack pack) and their Arlington Heights page is in the organic website results?

Below is the URL of the page from CorePower's website appears in the rankings. I've bolded the keywords from my search:

www.corepower**yoga**.com/**yoga-studios**/illinois/**arlington-heights/arlington-heights**

A key point here is that *this landing page has high quality content helpful to human viewers* versus a "thin" page of content that isn't helpful but which was developed exclusively for ranking in search engines.

When taking the approach of building out individual pages for different geographies, be careful that you are creating high-quality content so you don't get a quality penalty from Google.

In March 2015, Google published on its Google Webmaster Central blog[1] that "We have a long-standing view that doorway pages that are created solely for search engines can harm the quality of the user's search experience." There have been many websites that have received manual action penalties from Google for having doorway pages.

A "manual action penalty" is when Google's spam prevention team determines that you've broken too many of their rules and they remove you from the search results. This can typically happen if you practice spammy blackhat link building tactics, and also if you have super low quality content on your website.

A "doorway page" is a web page or website that is "thin" in content — meaning it has limited value to potential visitors and was designed purely to lure people in an redirect them to something else.

> Create content that actually adds value to your customers versus just "Doing SEO."

To avoid getting penalized and, more importantly, to actually add a valuable page of content that will generate business, focus on creating pages that are of high quality and not merely duplicates of other pages with only a new city name being targeted. While it may be tempting to copy and paste your "Plumbing" content into 35 new pages for 35 new cities and just replace the city name and nothing else — don't do it.

For more information on Local Landing Pages, check out Miriam Ellis' "Overcoming Your Fear of Local Landing Pages" post on the Moz Blog.[2]

Dos	Don'ts
Have unique, valuable, interesting content on each page	Do NOT use the same content on every swap out the content.... Unless you want duplicate content penalties
Photo contest! Have photos of your team across town in the area. At the parade, the coffee shop, etc. Be Local.	Do NOT use the sames stock photo on every location page and just change the file name.
Link to the pages visibly from the main menu/navigation and throughout the site.	Do NOT just stuff these pages in, bury them, and link to them from the footer in white font.
Mark up each page with review schema from each area.	Do NOT keyword stuff garbage + city info into each page. Garbage in = garbage out.

Local On-Page SEO Essentials

Now that you have an understanding of the strategy behind creating and optimizing individual pages of your website, it's time to look at the nitty gritty of what you need to update on each page with the On-Page Local SEO Essentials, described below.

According to the 2017 edition of the Moz Local Search Ranking Factors Survey,[3] On-page Signals represent about 14% of the ranking algorithm to get found in the Local Pack (map) results and 24% of the ranking algorithm to get found in the organic (list of ten webpage results beneath the maps). This means that this section of the book is pretty important!

Local Pack/Finder Ranking Factors

Localized Organic Ranking Factors

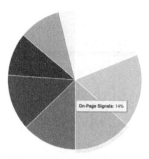

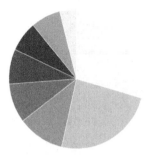

1. **My Business Signals** (Proximity, categories, keyword in business title, etc.) **19%**
2. **Link Signals** (Inbound anchor text, linking domain authority, linking domain quantity, etc.) **17%**
3. **On-Page Signals** (Presence of NAP, keywords in titles, domain authority, etc.) **14%**
4. **Citation Signals** (IYP/aggregator NAP consistency, citation volume, etc.) **13%**
5. **Review Signals** (Review quantity, review velocity, review diversity, etc.) **13%**

1. **Link Signals** (Inbound anchor text, linking domain authority, linking domain quantity, etc.) **29%**
2. **On-Page Signals** (Presence of NAP, keywords in titles, domain authority, etc.) **24%**
3. **Behavioral Signals** (Click-through rate, mobile clicks to call, check-ins, etc.) **11%**
4. **Personalization 9%**
5. **Citation Signals** (IYP/aggregator NAP consistency, citation volume, etc.) **8%**

Local Pack/Finder Ranking Factors

Localized Organic Ranking Factors

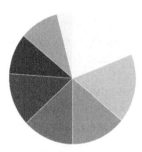

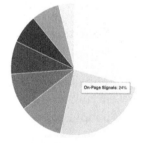

1. **My Business Signals** (Proximity, categories, keyword in business title, etc.) **19%**
2. **Link Signals** (Inbound anchor text, linking domain authority, linking domain quantity, etc.) **17%**
3. **On-Page Signals** (Presence of NAP, keywords in titles, domain authority, etc.) **14%**
4. **Citation Signals** (IYP/aggregator NAP consistency, citation volume, etc.) **13%**
5. **Review Signals** (Review quantity, review velocity, review diversity, etc.) **13%**

1. **Link Signals** (Inbound anchor text, linking domain authority, linking domain quantity, etc.) **29%**
2. **On-Page Signals** (Presence of NAP, keywords in titles, domain authority, etc.) **24%**
3. **Behavioral Signals** (Click-through rate, mobile clicks to call, check-ins, etc.) **11%**
4. **Personalization 9%**
5. **Citation Signals** (IYP/aggregator NAP consistency, citation volume, etc.) **8%**
6. **My Business Signals** (Proximity, categories, keyword in

(You can see the full survey at www.moz.com/local-search-ranking-factors)

Page Title Tags

> The page title tags are one of the single-most influential parts of on-page SEO.
> A page title is the title given to a document (a web page) and is edited in the HTML of the site. Page title tags show up in search results, shown below.

Your page title tag should:

- Absolutely include

  - Your target keyword at the start of the tag;

  - The city you are targeting (and/or state if your keyword research indicates many people search with a state modifier);

  - Up to 70 characters.

- Probably include (if there's room)

  - State abbreviation (especially if your city exists in multiple states, such as Springfield, Louisville, Lafayette, Jacksonville, etc.).

Here are two examples of well-optimized local SEO title tags:

URL: **www.larksbluegrass.com/**

Page Title: **Boulder Bluegrass Band | The Larks | Bluegrass Wedding Band Colorado**

Characters: **68**

Target keywords: **"Boulder Bluegrass band" "Bluegrass wedding band"**

Now, take a close look at the screenshots of the search results. Notice the title tags?

Search results for "Boulder bluegrass wedding band"

^^^Disclosure: This is my bluegrass band! Check us out at larksbluegrass.com.

Below is another example for a custom woodworking company.

URL: **www.jordanwoodworking.com/**

Page Title: **Longmont Custom Woodworking | Jordan Woodworking Boulder, CO**

Characters: **60**

Target keywords: **"Custom Woodworking" "Woodworking"**

Geographies: **Longmont, CO; Boulder, CO**

Search results for "woodworking Boulder CO"

You can test how your title tags will appear in the search results with Moz's title tag tester.[4]

Meta Description

The meta description is a short description of a webpage that includes up to 150 characters. The meta description does not directly influence rankings of a web page, but the text does appear in the search results and can influence your click-thru rate (CTR), which is the number of people who actually click through from the search results to your listing.

I recommend that you think of the meta description as a mini advertisement for the page. It should be benefit-oriented and "sell" someone on clicking through to the page.

A meta description should include:

- Mention of the keywords you're targeting;

- Mention of the city or state you are servicing;

- A phone number if you want people to call you from the description;

- A benefit-oriented description that answers "What's in it for me if I click on this?"

- Up to 300 characters.

In December of 2017, Google started showing much more of the meta descriptions in their snippets —

especially on mobile devices. Now, you can get away with longer, more descriptive meta descriptions which will in turn give you more real estate in the search engine results to potential customers. Still, keep them succinct, to the point, and written in a way that would entice someone browsing the web to click through to your webpage.

Example:

URL: **www.ramblinjackson.com/2016/07/15/cloud-backup-solution-mac-pc-video/**

Page title: **Best Cloud Backup Solution for Mac + PC**

Meta Description: **Is your business prepared for a fire or disaster? Watch today's video to learn how to backup your Mac + PC to keep your business up and running.**

And here's how it appears in the search results:

> Best Cloud Backup Solution for Mac + PC... - Ramblin Jackson
> www.ramblinjackson.com/2016/07/15/**cloud-backup**-solution-**pc**-video/ ▾
> Jul 15, 2016 - Is your business prepared for a fire or disaster? Watch today's video to learn how to
> **backup** your Mac + PC to keep your business up and ... ◄———— **Meta Description**

Keywords in URL

Use your target keyword plus your geographic modifier in your URLs. In the "wheel alignment madison WI" search example above, all but one of the results add the keywords in the URL. Don't get

too carried away here or your page can appear
spammy.

Search results for "wheel alignment Madison WI"

Wheel Alignment in Madison, WI | Capitol Tire And Service
captire.net/wheel-alignments-madison-wi ▼ ◄——————— **Keywords in URL**
Capitol Tire And Service offers quality Automotive Wheel Alignment in Madison, WI. Call us or Click
'Schedule Apt' to schedule your next service appointment ...

Caution: if you already have a web page that is
indexed and ranking well in Google, I would NOT
recommend editing it. Editing URLs can be very
risky if redirections are not handled properly. A
redirection is when an old URL points to a new
URL — kind of like when you update the post office
when you change your address. Learn more about
that at www.moz.com/learn/seo/redirection

Here's how we make the decision at Ramblin
Jackson:

- If it is a NEW PAGE that has not been
  published or a brand new website, include
  keywords in the URL.

- If it is an EXISTING PAGE that is already
  live on the internet and indexed in Google,
  do NOT edit the URL to include keywords.

- If you have to edit the URL and a 301
  Redirection is required, such as when
  there's an extension (e.g.,
  example.com/page.aspx, which changes to a
  new URL structure), then the new URL
  may contain keywords.

Use Keywords in H1, H2, and H3 Headings

Headings help organize blocks of text for readers. While the impact on rankings from using keywords in your headings has diminished over the years, headings help humans understand what your content is about and also help you organize your thoughts.

Think of the headlines in a newspaper. Before you decide to read an entire article, you'll quickly read the headline to determine if it's worth your time. Similarly, a heading can help people reading your page find the information they're looking for.

Headings come in hierarchical order on a webpage — H1 being the largest, then H2, then H3, and so on.

The H1 heading is the most important. It should include:

Your target keyword;

- Your city or state;

- Writing that clearly communicates a benefit and sounds great when read aloud.

Headings should NOT be exact match - which is when it's the exact keyword phrase you're optimizing for. Why? Because that's boring! Your headings should help answer *what's in it for me* AND help your page get found in search results.

I recommend that you also use H2 and H3 headings to break up the rest of your text. A good rule of thumb is to use a heading every 300 words.

Use Keyword Phrases Two to Three Times per Page

When writing your website text, do your best to use the keyword phrases two to three times on the page in as natural way as possible. Remember, *your website text is more for humans than it is for search engines.* If you write over-optimized garbage copy, it may rank... but no one will like reading it and they won't call you.

A tactic I like to use when writing local SEO copy is to have value statements featuring keywords in the headings, followed by a paragraph or bulleted list of descriptive copy.

SEO Tip: Use the Command F (Mac) or CTRL F (PC) feature on a web page or Google Doc to pull up the "Find in document" box to quickly highlight keywords in a page.

Command F pulls up the "Find in Document" box → dental crown
to help you count how many times you've used a keyword.

Restore Your Smile With Thornton's Top Provider for Dental Crowns, Dental Bridges, & Implant Restorations

Dental crowns, bridges, and implant restorations can help you restore cracked, chipped, or broken teeth. If you're looking to have a dentist in the Thornton area help you with this, we'd be happy to answer any questions you may have – so feel free to give us a call at (303) 284-6483!

What is a Dental Crown and Why Would You Need One?

A dental crown is often a great way to restore a broken or cracked tooth, or a tooth that's had a root canal. Oftentimes, once your old fillings are removed it will create a very fragile tooth that can no longer support a bigger filling; covering it with a crown or "cap" is recommended. The crown surrounds the whole tooth preventing it from further fracture and is cemented into place. Our crowns are made without the use of metals so no unsightly grey will show at your gumline.

Use Geographic Keywords for Cities, States, and Regions Served

In your website text, use your geographic keywords two to three times per page to help modify your keywords. Again, do this as naturally as possible, in a way that sounds good when read aloud.

Here are a few tactics for adding geographic keywords:

Located X miles from Y and Z - i.e., "Located just five blocks from the Blue Line stop at O'Hare International Airport and a 6-minute drive from downtown Rosemont or 15 minutes from Des Plaines, our restaurant is the most convenient place to get a quality slice of pizza before you hop on a plane!"

Directions from X city and Y city on Contact Page - i.e., "From Denver, head north on I-25 past Thornton. Exit at Y road in Northglenn... If you're coming from Westminster, head north on .... "

City's Best Keyword - i.e., "If you're looking for Seattle's best cioppino, you've come to the right place! People travel from Bellevue, Redmond, and all over Washington and beyond just to get this classic soup. See our specials page for more info."

Lead Readers to the Next Step with Calls to Action

The purpose of all of this on-page SEO is to get found by a potential customer *and have them contact you or come to your business.* What do you want people to *do*, specifically, when they visit your site? While the goal of your page will be different depending on your business and sales process, you should absolutely have strong, clear calls to action on every page to make it easy for people to take the next step in doing business with you.

Here are some examples calls to action for local businesses:

1. Call us today for a free consultation / book an appointment / make a reservation / etc.;

2. Get directions;

3. Fill out contact form/request a quote;

4. Download a white paper, etc.;

5. Purchase tickets;

6. Make a donation;

7. Register for an event/webinar.

Whatever the call to action is, make it clear, easy, and benefit-oriented. If you want people to join your mailing list, let them know "what's in it for me" if they give you their email address.

Internal Links

We'll discuss the importance of link building at greater length later in the chapter, but for the sake of on-page SEO you should try to link to other pages of your website. When one page of your site links to another, it's called an internal link.

Using internal links will help people viewing your site discover other pages of your website and new services that they may not otherwise know about. It also helps the pages being linked increase their rank in search results.

When linking to other pages in your site, use the title of that page in the **anchor text** of the link. Anchor text is the highlighted text that appears in a link on a webpage.

Examples with the internal links:

For a dentist website: "In addition to family dentistry, we also offer **teeth whitening** to help brighten your smile."

For a tire shop website: "At Bob's Tires, our mission is to help you enjoy driving as safely and smoothly as possible. Not only do we offer the best prices on new tires in Madison, we also help keep your car straight with affordable **wheel alignment services**."

Optimized Footer

The footer of your website is a great opportunity for optimized content. The footer is a global website setting that shows up on every page of your website at the bottom.

Your footer should include:

- **Business Name, Address, & Phone Number**
  - ***** Phone Number format: (XXX) XXX-XXXX
    - NOT XXX.XXX.XXXX
      - the dots are cute, but not optimized
    - Formatting is critical to match Google My Business listings formatting
- **Store hours** - if you are a retail business
- **Helpful links to prominent pages**
- **Other options:**
  - Lead generation form or call-to-action button

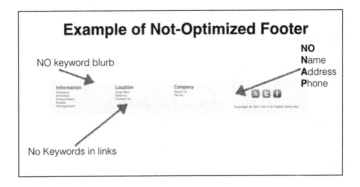

Like anything else with SEO, be careful not to over-optimize your footer with a billion different cities that you service and way too many links. If it looks gross, it probably is. Especially if you're, say, a locksmith in...

Hoover City, NV

Bonanza Village, NV

North Las Vegas, NV

Vegas Heights, NV

Eastland Heights, NV

Winchester, NV

Wann, NV

Sunrise Manor, NV

Winterwood, NV

Paradise, NV

Bracken, NV

Hillegas, NV

Boulder Junction, NV

Spring Valley, NV

East Las Vegas, NV

Valley, NV

Whitney, NV

Help Search Engines Understand Your Business with Schema

Google makes money from Maps and Search when people a) see Google Adwords advertisements and/or b) click on Google Adwords advertisements.

When you do a search in Google and click on a website or map result, *you leave Google and they stop making money from you (*unless you click onto a site which they own or advertise on, like YouTube). So, they are constantly trying to find ways to be the best search engine, give you what you want, AND keep you clicking on or seeing advertisements.

One of the things that Google is doing to keep you *in* the search results is answer your question entirely without requiring you to leave. Take the search results for "how to fry an egg" as an example. See how above the website results they actually list out the instructions with a photo? You don't even need to leave the search results!

Here are three examples of how Google is doing
this in local searches:

1. If you search for "best," i.e., "best burgers
   boulder," it will automatically sort your map
   results based on the businesses selling
   burgers that have the highest review
   averages. Additionally, it will show you the
   review averages from other review sites
   such as Facebook, Yelp, Tripadvisor, etc.
   right under the Google My Business listing
   *without requiring you to leave Google search
   results to see their information.*

2. If you search for "open now" i.e., "bars near
   me open now" it will automatically sort your
   results based on the businesses who have
   open store hours that are near you.

3. If you search "top lawyers in kansas city"
    Google is pulling the results from a
    superlawyers.com article right into the
    search results into its "Knowledge Graph."

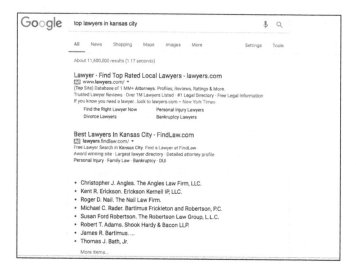

More and more, Google is *scraping data from your website and directories* and displaying it in its Knowledge Graph. I like how David Mihm, a prominent writer on the topic of SEO and marketing, coaches people to think of their website as an API from which Google pulls information and displays it in its search results.

Search engines like Google, Yahoo, Bing, and Yandex (a Russian search engine) all use an open source code called schema to help display more visually interesting attributes in the search results, like the list of recipes or list of top lawyers shown above. One type of schema you can use is called **JSON-LD**, which stands for or JavaScript Object Notation for Linked Data, is a method of encoding Linked Data using JSON.

This section isn't meant to be a full tutorial, but more to make you aware of schema and that you should have it. You can learn more about schema by visiting Google's developer site: www.developers.google.com/search/docs/data-types/local-businesses.

Here are a few things you could include in your schema to help search engines display your information in search results (potentially instead of your competitors who aren't doing this!):

- Business Name

- Address

- Phone

- Opening hours

- Price range

- Geo-coordinates

- Accepts Reservations

There's a whole lot more you can mark up. The trend is that you can **take action from the search results** more and more versus clicking through to a website to take action. Just like you can search and book a flight from the search results, you can now book a reservation at a restaurant, schedule a yoga class, and more.

In the medical and dental fields, there are integrations available from companies like ZocDocs and HealthGrades where you can schedule an appointment right from the Google My Business listing. If you're looking for a urologist in Chattanooga, Tennessee, for example, you could book an appointment right from his Google listing:

Increasingly, SEO is much more than just getting found. It's about being found *and making yourself accessible to your customers on their terms.*

Links: The Missing Link between Good Rankings and Great Rankings

There are over 90 trillion pages in Google's index. Holy Best Burgers Toledo, Batman.

How should Google prioritize which ones are on their first page let alone in which order on the first page?

As I mentioned earlier in the first part on Local SEO, Google determines local ranking based on relevance, distance, and prominence. While much of this chapter has focused on making your website and online directories relevant through consistent, complete NAP citations and by using correct keywords in on-page optimization, this next section will address the topic of prominence.

Let's say that there are 25 cosmetic dentists in the city of Cleveland, Ohio. Each of them have consistent NAP citations, solid on-page SEO, and quality websites that load quickly and display well on mobile devices. How would search engines determine which of them should rank for the search query, "cosmetic dentists Cleveland Ohio?"

One of the ways that Google makes this determination is to evaluate the number and quality of links pointing to the websites.

PageRank

In the beginning, Google called this part of its ranking algorithm PageRank — a double entendre consisting of the name of Google's co-founder, Larry Page, and then a web pages position in the search results. The PageRank algorithm evolved over the years to include not only the number of links pointing to a page but also the *quality* of the links pointing to a site or page based on the PageRank of the linking site and its relevance.

Domain Authority: A Metric for Measuring the Quantity and Quality of Links

Google later stopped updating PageRank scores because SEOs were spamming it. Links are still a significant part of the algorithm — they just don't tell you your current PageRank score anymore. Moz developed a score called Domain Authority that expands the PageRank score to incorporate other factors, including a spam score.

Domain Authority, also called DA, is a score (based on a 100-point scale) developed by Moz that predicts how well a website will rank on search engines. Domain Authority is the industry standard for measuring the "strength" of websites over time. Moz calculates this metric by combining all of our other link metrics — linking root domains, number of total links, MozRank, MozTrust, etc. — into a single score. For reference, on the very high end, a site like huffingtonpost.com has a Domain Authority of 98.

Domain Authority will vary quite a bit for local businesses. The more populated and competitive a market, such as in a city like Chicago or Houston, the higher the Domain Authority you'll likely need to rank highly.

Aside from Domain Authority, *each Page* of a website has its own **Page Authority,** which is influenced by the number and quality of links (both internal links from within the site and external links) pointing to it.

You can see your Domain Authority, and compare it to some of your competition, with Moz's free Open Site Explorer tool.[5]

Links Represent Trust

Think about this: Why would you ever link someone *off* of your website after you've done so much work to get them there? You would only do so if you knew that it was trustworthy and would be helpful to someone viewing your site. That's why Google values links so highly: They represent humans endorsing other humans (who operate websites).

Five Link-Building Ideas for Local Businesses

1. Chamber of Commerce Directory

Your local Chamber of Commerce will have a directory. It'll have a nice mention of your name, address, phone number, and a business description.

I've been a chamber member for seven years. The Boulder Chamber has been amazing. I get a ton of value from it, from networking and speaking to actually showing up and doing stuff. I get a domain authority 57 link pointing to my website — and I get leads from it.

Your Chamber of Commerce can be really powerful. Even if you don't go to stuff, get a link. If your competitors aren't in your town and you have a thriving Chamber of Commerce, your competitor probably won't get that link.

2. Industry-Specific Directories

There is a directory, ColoradoBluegrass.com, that has a list of bands on call. If you're looking to hire a bluegrass band, this is the place to go.

What are the industry directories for your business? Do a search for whatever your keyword is + directory and you'll find a bunch of them.

Watch Out For Skeezy Directories That Provide No Value To Humans

---

I recommend directories that provide value to humans, i.e. real websites that real humans would use. I do NOT recommend "link directories" that exist purely for the purpose of generating links for SEO purposes.

Here's an example of a bad link directory: DenverMetrolinks.com. Seriously, what *is* DenverMetrolinks.com? What do you even do on this website? If you ever see a website that has like a spider web and like a pirate GIF, that's skeezy. Do not get a link there. If you wouldn't send your mom to the website, don't do it. If you can just submit to the site, gross. Stay away from there.

3. Vendors, Partners, Etc.

Where are your expenses going? Who are you spending money with that you have a relationship? Absolutely get a link from their website.

4. Write a Testimonial

Who do you do business with that would love a testimonial? Write up a testimonial for their website, and ask them to add your name and a link back to your website along with it. Boom.

5. Get Creative

There are a lot of other ways to build links for your business. You could create a really helpful blog post, guide, or infographic, and reach out to people to link to it. You could get interviewed on podcasts and have people link to you that way. You could donate in-kind services to nonprofits or other organizations and get links that way. You could even get links from your college website... maybe. The key is to <u>get links that your competitors don't have by leveraging your relationships with humans who manage websites.</u>

Additional SEO Resources

This is just the tip of the iceberg for SEO. There's so much more! If you've enjoyed this content, here are some other resources you might enjoy too:

1. Google Webmaster Tools' Search Engine Optimization (SEO) Starter Guide – www.support.google.com/webmasters/answer/7451184

2. Moz Beginner's Guide To SEO www.moz.com/beginners-guide-to-seo

3. Whiteboard Friday www.moz.com/blog

Sign up for my weekly sales and marketing video series, Friday's Ramblin Roundup, at ramblinjackson.com/roundup/

Key Takeaways From How To Get Found By Your Perfect Customers With Local SEO - Part 2

- Have your website developer mark up your site for local schema.

- Google ranks web pages, not websites.

- Build high quality links for your website regularly.

- Create content that actually adds value to your customers versus just doing SEO.

7

ARE YOU THE BEST?
BECOME THE CHOICE
WITH STRONG REVIEWS

"You can't build a reputation on
what you are going to do."

- Henry Ford

There is nothing better than referrals. No matter
what business you're in, you know that getting a
new customer, client, or patient as a result of a
referral is a good thing. It means that you have
done a great job for your client and that they're
happy enough to endorse you.

What many local business owners don't realize is
that getting online reviews is equally as important
as getting referrals, if not more.

If you get a referral, chances are that person is going to do some online research about your business. It could be as simple as them Googling your business name or looking up your location, directions, or store hours on Google Maps, Yelp, or Apple Maps. They'll undoubtedly encounter reviews — good or bad — which could sway their decision to follow through on the referral.

Reviews also have increasing influence on your rankings in search engine results and, more importantly, on influencing real purchasing decisions.

In this chapter, you'll not only learn why reviews are important to running a local business but also where and how to get them.

Reviews Influence
Search Engine Rankings

"Google review count and score are factored into local search ranking: more reviews and positive ratings will probably improve a business's local ranking," says Google, referring to Google My Business listings.[1]

Note that Google says it "will probably improve" your ranking — but I'll tell you from first-hand experience working with hundreds of businesses, it DOES.

Here are a few things that happen when you get reviews on your Google My Business Listing:

- After you get three reviews (or in some cases even two reviews), gold stars show up next to your listing in the search results;

- People are visually drawn to the listings with gold stars and, if you have them, they'll be more likely to click on your listing;

- People will perceive your business as better than the businesses without stars;

- People will likely spend more time on your website. Having people click onto your site influences your click-thru rate (which is the percentage of people who click onto a site or listing from the search results). Increasing your CTR can increase your rankings;

- People will trust your business more and be more likely to call you and, ultimately, buy from you.

Reviews are powerful! Boom. Go get three gold star reviews. Easy peasy, right?

Reviews Influence Search Results for "Best" Queries

One trend I've seen continue over the last few years is an increase in the amount of searches with "best" in the query. It now impacts Google's ranking algorithm as a result.

Here is the Google Trends[2] data for the query, "best wings near me."

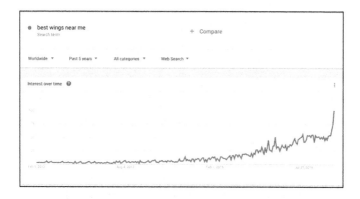

And here are the search results (taken from my MacBook Air using Google Chrome from Lyons, Colorado).

When I add "best" to the query, Google shows me South Mouth Wings, which is 16.2 miles away, as the third listing, even though Domino's Pizza is only 11.1 miles away. That's because South Mouth Wings has a rating average of 3.6 whereas Domino's Pizza has a 2.9.

Reviews matter... and here's why:

According to Mike Blumenthal, a highly-respected local search thought leader and co-founder of GetFiveStars, a customer ratings and reviews platform, reviews on a Google My Business listing result in a 140% increase in driving directions and a 350% increase in website visits from the local search results. Not surprisingly, his advice to small businesses was "get more reviews."

Blumenthal said there are two paths businesses can take to accomplish that goal: active and passive.

"The active path involves asking every customer for feedback while the passive approach relies on the use of listening posts, such as social media," he said. "I recommend a combination of the two. Customer feedback is valuable whether it comes in the form of a complaint or compliment, so find as many ways to get it as you can."

Reviews Influence Purchase Decisions

While increasing your ranking in Google is all good and gravy, what really matters is that people *choose to do business with you* over the other businesses they find online. That's how you put more money in the bank.

Each year, BrightLocal, a company that specializes in local search, conducts the Local Consumer Review Survey.[3] Here are the key takeaways from their 2016 report, which surveyed 1,062 individuals on a U.S.-based consumer panel:

1. 84% of people trust online reviews as much as a personal recommendation;

2. 7 out of 10 consumers will leave a review for a business if they're asked to;

3. 90% of consumers read less than 10 reviews before forming an opinion about a business;

4. 54% of people will visit the website after reading positive reviews;

5. 73% of consumers think that reviews older than 3 months are no longer relevant;

6. 74% of consumers say that positive reviews make them trust a local business more;

7. 58% of consumers say that the star rating of a business is most important.

Consumer Trust in Online Reviews on the Rise

BrightLocal has been doing this survey each year since 2010 and, as a result, have been able to spot some trends. One fact their surveys reveal:

customer reviews have a mounting influence on purchasing decisions.

"A significant 85% of consumers trust online reviews as much as personal recommendations if they meet criteria such as number of reviews or type of business. This has risen from 84% in 2016," according to the survey.[4]

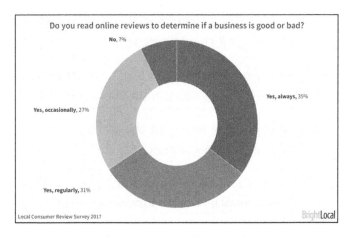

Do you read online reviews to determine if a business is good or bad?

No, 7%

Yes, always, 35%

Yes, occasionally, 27%

Yes, regularly, 31%

Local Consumer Review Survey 2017   BrightLocal

Reviews from the Web

I've found that many businesses focus *only* on getting Google reviews. While having reviews on your Google My Business listing is certainly important, it is also necessary to have reviews on a variety of review sites. Not only will people read your reviews on other sites, Google will pull those reviews into your Google My Business listing.

In September of 2016, Google introduced Reviews from the Web,[5] a feature where it aggregates reviews from other websites.

"Available globally on mobile and desktop, Reviews from the web brings aggregated user ratings of up to three review sites to Knowledge Panels for local places across many verticals including shops, restaurants, parks and more."

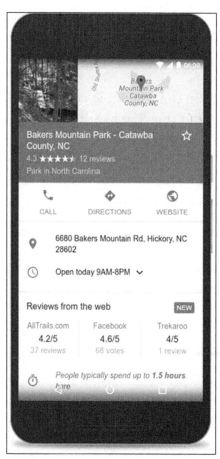

The Words Used in Reviews Affect Google Rankings

Not only does the quantity of the reviews that you have online influence your ranking, the text content of the reviews — especially those posted on other sites like Yelp, YellowPages, TripAdvisor, and so on — can actually influence your ranking in Google as well.

GetFiveStars' Blumenthal mentioned in his presentation at MozCon Local 2017, a conference all about local SEO, that he and a friend used the words "dive bar" in their Yelp reviews for 3rd Base, a sports bar in the small town of Olean, New York. Before they did this, the bar did not rank in Google for the query, "dive bar olean, NY." (There is no Google category for dive bar.) After they wrote the reviews, 3rd Base ranked in Google's knowledge graph for "dive bar Olean, NY."

My Famous Chicken Wings Experiment

I did a similar experiment in Colorado. I gave a presentation of "FOUND: How To Increase Sales With Local SEO" at the Boulder SEO Meetup, which took place at a sports bar called Mudrock's Tap & Tavern in Louisville, Colorado.

The Meetup leader and host of the SEO conference SearchCon, Jim Kreinbrink, and I each ate chicken wings for dinner. I observed that Mudrock's didn't rank for "chicken wings louisville CO", so Jim and I each wrote a review for them on Yelp mentioning "chicken wings." A month later, Mudrock's Tap & Tavern ranked in the local pack for "chicken wings Louisville CO."

What was even more fascinating to me was that their Google My Business short description that shows up for "chicken wings Louisville co" says "mom-&-pop sports bar known for wings" and when you Google their brand name "Mudrocks Tap & Tavern," their short description says: "Family-owned haunt with wings & other bar food, plus many regional craft beers & TVs showing sports.

Rankings before adding Yelp reviews:

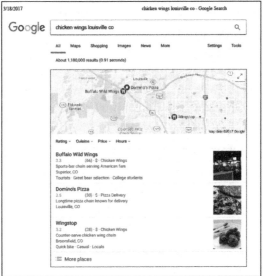

Rankings after adding Yelp reviews:

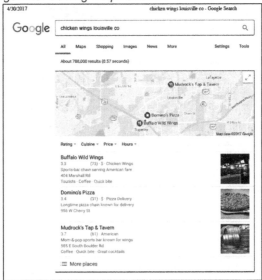

How to Find Out
Where to Get Reviews

We know that reviews influence purchasing decisions and that they influence your search engine rankings. But *where* do you need to get them? The answer will vary depending on your business type.

To find out on which directories you need to get reviews, take the following two steps:

1. Conduct a Google Search for Your Keyword + City

For example, search Google for "plumbing companies tuscaloosa, AL".

Which directories show up?

If you search something like "restaurants san diego," you'll likely find Google My Business, Yelp, Zagat, TripAdvisor, and Foursquare.

If you search "handyman bend OR," results could include Google My Business, Yelp, Angie's List, Home Advisor, and Yellow Pages.

Whatever your business is, look at the search results for your target keyword + city name and focus on getting reviews on the directories that appear on the first page. If you see a competitor ranking for your keyword, take a look at their Google My Business listing. Which sites are pulled into their "Reviews from the web" section?

2. Conduct a Google Search for Your Brand Name

Type your business name into Google along with the city name and state abbreviation. I.e. *Bob's Plumbing Powerhouse Tuscaloosa, AL*. What do you see? What are the top ranking/ most prominent directories that are ranking on page one? It's best to have reviews/stars showing on as many of those as possible. Do you have stars? Good stars? No stars?

Consider this: If you do print advertising, or any advertising for that manner, people will likely google your business name as part of looking up your phone number, location, etc. — and when they do, they will see reviews.

Do the reviews help or hinder their decision to do business with you? It's possible that the direct mail campaign just isn't working. But it's also possible negative online reviews are the problem

Check out the results when you google "Firehaus Pilates":

See how Yelp is the first listing under their website? It has visible stars and a 4.8 average with 13 reviews. Nice. Then there's a Groupon beneath it, and then Facebook, which also has stars and a 4.9 rating with 16 votes. The business' Facebook rating also shows up in the "Reviews from the web" section of the Knowledge Panel, beneath their 16 Google reviews with a 4.9 average. They look legit. Does your business look this good?

According to BrightLocal's Review Survey in 2017, Yelp and Facebook are the most trusted review sites for US consumers, followed by the BBB and Google. From my experience, certain regions of the country use some directories more than others. On the west coast, Yelp is used a bit more than say Angie's List is used in Ohio. This is why I recommend having reviews in a variety of places

and doing searches for the places where you need
them outlined above.

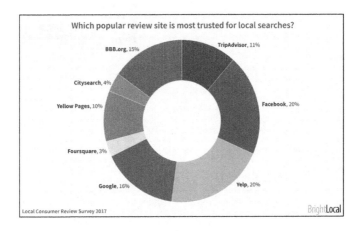

Gain Competitive Advantage
with Rating Schema

Minneapolis Glass Company: Custom Designed Residential ...
www.minneapolisglass.com/ ▾
Minneapolis Glass Company, a regional architectural glass fabricator located ... Glass Replacement
in Windows & Doors · Tempered & Laminated Safety Glass ...

Windshield Repair & Replacement in Minneapolis, MN | Safelite ...
https://www.safelite.com/stores/minneapolis ▾ Safelite ▾
★★★★✫ Rating: 4.6 - 208 reviews
Windshield Repair and Replacement in Minneapolis, MN ... You can also get full windshield
replacement at our Minneapolis auto glass center or call for an ...

Best Home window glass replacement in Minneapolis, MN - Yelp
https://www.yelp.com/search?find...glass+replacement...Minneapolis%2C... ▾ Yelp ▾
Reviews on Home window glass replacement in Minneapolis, MN - Glass Today, Scott's Window's &
Doors, LLC, Besser Glass & Mirror, Rapid Glass, Wellington ...

Above is a screenshot of the Google search results
for "Minneapolis glass repair." Which result is most
interesting? Which company looks best? If you
think it's the second listing, for
safelite.com/stores/minneapolis, you're like many
consumers.

The cool stars and rating included is a result of something called rating "schema,"[6] which is a code that your SEO specialist or web developer can add to your website that will display rating stars in your search engine results. This will help you stand out from your competitors and can lead to more clicks (and customers) as a result. (For a more technical definition of schema, check out the website, schema.org)

Be careful! Google has very specific rules about schema, and if you don't follow them perfectly, Google could block your site from the search results. You used to be able to just mark up your website with schema using ratings from other websites. But now, *the reviews must be written ON* your website by consumers. You can't add the reviews to the site — the customer must. GetFiveStars has this feature built in, and, at the time of this writing, it is compliant with the Google schema ratings requirements.

How to Respond to Negative Reviews without Sounding like a Jerk

Do you ever see businesses with negative reviews that go unanswered? What kind of message does that send to you as a potential customer?

Does the business care about its customers, or not? Has that owner totally checked out? What happens if I have a bad experience? Will they take care of me?

If you have negative reviews, it's critical that you respond to them. Just be careful with how you reply because you can come off sounding like a major d-bag.

Here are a few tips for how to respond to negative reviews:

1. Take a deep breath. Drink some coffee. Clear your head. Don't sound defensive or snotty.

First, it's nearly inevitable — you're going to get a bad review. It's not a matter of *if* but *when*. You're human. Your staff are humans. Your customers are human. And some of those humans are just plain rotten. Someone is going to screw up, make a mistake, or become upset. When that happens, it will likely end up online in the form of a review.

An initial reaction by most business owners is to get upset. The mistake they make is to hastily post a response to the review that has a negative or snarky tone. This can be worse, in my opinion, because it makes it look like a) not only did the business screw up but also b) when they do screw up, they're going to be difficult about it.

That's why I recommend taking a deep breath, calming down, and cooling your head before taking next steps. A negative review is actually a tremendous PR opportunity.

Having a few bad reviews isn't actually a bad thing! A study from PowerReviews and

Northwestern University[7] concluded that consumers are more likely to trust reviews with a rating between 4.2 and 4.5. Having all 5-star reviews sounds a little suspicious... Did they just have their friends and family reply?

2. Verify that this is actually from a real customer.

One time, one of my clients, Flatirons Carpet and Hardwood Cleaning, received a negative review on their Google listing from a grumpy customer who said that they missed an appointment and then were late to the next one. I wrote the bio for this business and remembered that the owner, Mike Finnesy, was an Eagle Scout who valued being on-time more than anyone I'd ever met. It's all over the website as a unique selling proposition because people in the carpet cleaning industry are notoriously late.

I knew right away the review was either fake or written for the wrong business. The Flatirons are a popular mountain range in Boulder, and there are many businesses with "Flatirons" in their business name. I gave this person the benefit of the doubt and assumed they were accidentally reviewing the wrong business.

Here's the response we posted:

> *"We don't have any record of working with someone with your name, and we think you might be mistaking us with another company in*

Lafayette that has the same name as us. They do not have their business listed here on Google, so you may have found us accidentally. At Flatirons Carpet & Hardwood Cleaning, punctuality and quality work are the driving forces of our business, and we can assure you that you would not have this problem had you hired us. We respectfully ask that you confirm the business you hired, and if it was not us, please remove your review. If you have additional problems, please call us right away -- (303) 443-0318. Sincerely, Mike Finnesy, Owner of Flatirons Carpet & Hardwood Cleaning. "

That day, Mike got a call from the guy who confirmed that he was confusing Mike's business with another one. He apologized and promptly took down the review.

I see this happen all the time!

If you verify that it IS your customer, promptly post a response acknowledging the issue, apologize, and leave your phone number asking the person to call you. This shows the public that you're at least listening and trying to help.

3. Pick up the telephone and call your customer. Settle the matter offline.

Once you've verified that it is actually your customer, talk with your staff and find out what happened. What went wrong and why is the customer upset?

Then, CALL them. Yes, on the telephone, so they can hear your human voice and you can hear theirs. (Shocking advice from a digital marketing guy, right?!)

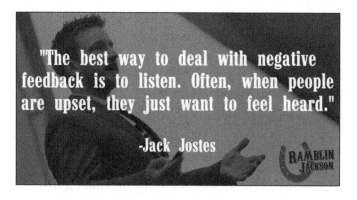

"The best way to deal with negative feedback is to listen. Often, when people are upset, they just want to feel heard."

-Jack Jostes

Most of the time, people just want to complain. They want to vent. They want to _feel_ heard.

If you genuinely listen to an upset client or customer, they will really appreciate it. A lot of the times, you can talk with people, make it up to them (offer a free appetizer or something), calm them down, and ask them to remove the review.

This tip was featured in Inc. Magazine: How Should You React To Criticism.[8]

4. Post a reply. Have someone else proofread it first.

If you reach out to your customer or prospect and are unable to connect with them, post a response that makes mention of that fact. Perhaps your first response will suffice.

In any case, avoid being overly defensive, nasty, or having a "tone."

Sometimes, the customer is wrong. Sometimes, the customer is downright nasty. But if you reply with a tone that suggests that, it will send the wrong message to your prospective customers.

Be factual, be approachable, and let them know that you take the review seriously. Always have someone else proofread your reply to make sure that it adds value versus positioning your company as difficult to deal with.

5. Drink a cold root beer, move on, and get more reviews.

After you've taken these steps, it's probably time to have a cold beverage of your choice. It's already 7:37 p.m., you're still at work, and you let this eat up way more if your attention and time than you intended. Stop working. Don't worry too much about it. If your company screwed up, figure out how you can systematically prevent this same issue from happening again. Let your staff know how you handled it. Then, focus on earning more good reviews!

How to Get Reviews

One of the best ways to get reviews is to *ask* for them.

When people are in your store or shop telling you what a great experience they had, it's the perfect time to say, "Mary, I'm so glad you've enjoyed working with us. As a small business owner, it would mean the world to me if you share that online. Would you do me a favor and write a review on Google?"

Mary will say, "Of course! I'll be happy to." Mary has mostly good intentions and is, for the most part, a decent person who may actually want to help you. Except that after she leaves your business, she picks up her kids from soccer practice. They are yelling and screaming in the car and she forgets all about you. Later, Mary has a glass of wine and goes to bed — and you have no Google review.

Instead, *ask Mary to take out her phone and do it before she leaves.* Do this politely, delicately, and without being skeezy. If you do it correctly, Mary will write a quick review right on the spot.. (She probably already used Google Maps to get to your business anyway.)

Say something like, "Mary, thanks for offering to do this. Do you have Google Maps on your phone?

You can search for our company name and write a quick review."

You NEED to ask people to write reviews. Unless you're a restaurant — which is an industry where consumers are more prone to write reviews — you'll have to proactively request reviews and let people know that you'd value it if they did. Otherwise, they probably won't think of it.

Here are a few ways to do this:

1. **Print postcards or flyers.** Have a print postcard or flyer at your point of sale that requests reviews. My dentist offers a discount if you check-in and write a review on Facebook. I did it and thanked him for the reminder. One time I got my car detailed. They did a great job and left a print door hanger from my rear view mirror with instructions on letting my car dry properly. THAT would have been a golden opportunity to ask for a review!

2. **Add a reviews page on your website and/or icons linking to your directory profiles.** Create a page on your website that has some testimonials and links to your review sites. This can make it easy for people to find or to reference in print, i.e. visit mydomainname.com/reviews. You can optimize the title tag for "Best <Keyword>

<City Name> | Brand Name Reviews" so people may find that page easily as well.

3. **Personally email a request to individuals.** I've found that the best way to get reviews for many businesses is a personal email to a customer. "Dear Bob, thanks for SOMETHING SPECIFIC THAT YOU DID WITH BOB." Ask for the review and insert the link.

4. **Post on social media** Post links to your review sites from your social media channels.

5. **Use review automation software.** There are programs out there that can automate a lot of this for you. I find GetFiveStars to be the best and recommend using them.

Why Are My Yelp Reviews "Not Recommended?"

Did you recently get some sweet reviews from your favorite customers... only to notice they weren't showing up anymore a week or so later? Chances are they're hidden in the "not recommended" section on your Yelp profile... But why? What can you do about it?

Yelp Filters Reviews — And It's Actually a Good Thing

Yelp filters their reviews. In my opinion, it's a good thing, or at least a good attempt at mitigating fake reviews — because this way only reviews from active Yelpers are shown (vs. reviews from business owner's friends who may not be actual customers or whose reviews may be biased base on their relationship). This makes the reviews on Yelp as a whole more credible, which in turn increases Yelp's value proposition in the market. If more people use/trust Yelp then the Advertising Yelp sells will be more valuable to small business owners.

No, you can't pay yelp for advertising to show them. Check out Yelp's FAQ for more information about this.

What to Do About It?
Get Good Reviews from Active Yelpers!

Now that you know why Yelp filters out some of your reviews, it's time to stop whining and focus on getting reviews from active Yelpers.

Before you spend a bunch of time asking your best customers to write reviews on Yelp -- you'll need to make sure you're asking people who are active on Yelp. This adds complexity to the process of getting reviews, but can help save you some heartache of bothering your top customers and persuading them to write a review on Yelp only to discover that their review is "Not Recommended."

Yelp Review Tip: Login to Facebook at the same time as Yelp to see which of your Friends in your network are active yelpers, and reach out to them there. See a video of this Yelp trick at ramblinjackson.com/yelptrick/

Additionally, you can post Yelp and other review site stickers in your print materials, like your flyers, receipts, invoices, etc., or even on the mirror in your bathroom if you're a brick and mortar, etc.

Automate Review Collection as Part of Your Sales Process with GetFiveStars

One of the great things about using GetFiveStars, the rating and review platform, is that you can automate the entire review collection process. Collecting reviews should be part of every sales process. Depending on your business, it will make sense to reach out at different times to different people, and using a program like GetFiveStars makes it much easier.

With GetFiveStars, you can import your database from another site, such as MailChimp, Constant Contact, or your point of sale system, and then send review requests to your customers.

You can direct recipients to a page on your site
where they can give feedback. If they give you a
three out of five star or above average, it will can
display automatically on your site. If people give
you a review that's lower than three stars, you can
collect more information and be notified that you
need to follow up. It can also redirect them to
whichever review sites you are trying to use to
collect reviews.

The best part, the software will automatically
follow up with people who haven't opened the
emails or have yet to write a review. This solves
one of the most time-intensive parts of collecting
reviews — following up and getting them.

Additionally, GetFiveStars can add schema code
(referred to earlier) to your website that is
compliant with the Google rating schema standard.

Get a 30-Day Money-Back Guarantee from GetFiveStars at www.getfivestars.com/ramblin

The primary reason I endorse GetFiveStars is
because it was co-founded by Mike Blumenthal,
who is regarded as the godfather of local SEO.
Mike has worked with hundreds of businesses and
knows the challenges they face when it comes to
getting high search engine rankings. As a result,
he has learned firsthand the power reviews can
have.

Post a Rating or Review
of this book on Amazon!

If you've found this book to be helpful to
your business -- or even if you haven't --
I'd sure appreciate it if you'd give me an
honest review or rating on Amazon.

1) Visit Amazon.com -- right now --
on your smartphone or computer

2) Search "jack jostes get found online"

3) Click on my book

4) Scroll down to the
Customer Reviews section

5) Click "write a customer review" +
tell me what you think!

See what I did there? :)

Key Takeaways From Are You The Best? Become THE Choice With Strong Reviews

- Reviews influence your rankings in search engine results.

- Reviews have an increasing influence on purchase decisions and are trusted by many consumers as much as referrals.

- Having a few negative reviews is OK (as long as you have more good ones).

- Respond to negative reviews carefully. Have someone else proofread your response.

- You need reviews in many places, not just Google.

- Ask and ye shall receive! Don't be afraid to ASK your customers for reviews.

8

DRIVE REPEAT BUSINESS WITH EMAIL MARKETING

"Make new friends, but keep the old;
Those are silver, these are gold."

- Joseph Parry

As a small business owner or entrepreneur, you will always need to acquire new customers to replace those who, for whatever reason, no longer do business with you. Customers can die, change, become dissatisfied with you and your company, move, get divorced, have kids, run out of money, go out of business, no longer need your product or service, become a bad customer, and otherwise need to be replaced. Problems arise, however, when you become so focused on expanding your customer base that you lose sight of your most important asset: your existing customers.

At the Local Search Association's 2016 Annual Conference, Google shared that it costs five to ten times more to sign up a new customer than it does to retain an existing one.[1] Google also said that selling to existing customers has a 60-70% probability of success, compared to only 5 to 20% for new customers.

People who have had a good experience with your business:

- Have already done all of the research to choose you instead of a competitor;

- Will be more likely to refer business to you;

- Will be more likely to write an online review for you;

- Will spend more with you;

- Should be treated differently.

One of the best ways to drum up repeat business from your existing clientele, in addition to calling them on the telephone, is by utilizing one of the most traditionally-accepted, cost-effective, forms of digital marketing: email.

In this chapter, I outline some of the benefits and ways to use email to drive repeat business.

Three Reasons Why Email Works

Email isn't sexy. Email may not be cool. But by golly, email works. Here are three reasons why:

1. **Email is a universally accepted form of communication.** According to a Radicati Group study, by the end of 2021, the number of worldwide email users will be over 4.1 billion. That means that nearly 54% of the entire planet currently uses email.

2. **You own your email data.** You do not own your Facebook Likes; Facebook does. If Facebook closed down, you would lose all of your followers. You do not own your Google rankings either. By contrast, *you* own your email database. If your email marketing company peaces out, no problem. Just export that database, choose a new email marketing company, upload your list, and you're off and running.

3. **Email is the preferred form of marketing communication.** I see a lot of garbage online that "email is dead." I talk with many businesses who falsely assume that because text messaging has grown as a means of personal communication, it has replaced email.

Personally, I can't stand to receive text messages from businesses — and I'm not alone.

A 2015 survey of 6,000 people by Yodle,[2] an online marketing platform, found that email is, by far, the preferred method of communication among customers of local businesses (69%) when compared to other forms of marketing, including text messaging (7%).

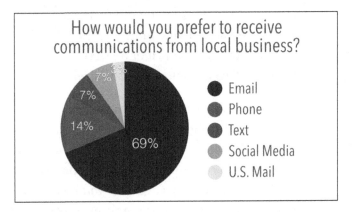

Moreover, "80% of marketers agree that email is core to their business," said Salesforce in its 2016 State of Marketing Report.[3]

How Flatirons Carpet and Hardwood Got 10 Jobs within the First Hour of One Email Campaign

Like I mentioned in the Reviews chapter, many businesses in the Boulder area reference the popular mountain range "the Flatirons" in their business name. Such is the case for my friends and clients, Mike and Becky, who run Flatirons Carpet and Hardwood, the same folks who had the bad review posted by someone who had mistaken them for another company.

Their business does carpet, hardwood, and upholstery cleaning. Many times, people find the company on Google when they have an emergency, such as a pet stain or when someone spills wine on their couch, and need to have it removed right away.

In the past, Flatirons would show up on time, like they promised, do a great job, and move on to the next job. For many years, however, there was little in the way of follow-up with customers after the service was performed, and they were not collecting email addresses. Because their business name was similar to many others in the area, it's likely that the people who found them on Google for an emergency service would forget about them later on.

We started helping Mike and Becky collect email addresses for each customer. This resulted in improved cash flow because they could send invoices via email and follow up with people so they could pay online through a link contained in the message.

We also started sending a quarterly email newsletter to their existing customer base. Because they also own another business — Your Sprinkler Guy, which provides irrigation services — we would cross promote the two. We always made sure to include photos of Mike and Becky, the company logo, and other branding, so people remembered who they were receiving email from.

The messages were simple and included a cleaning or yard maintenance tip and a casual but direct response offer — if you responded by a certain date you could get a discount on a service.

We turned the messaging around at certain times of the year when people might need the services: change of season, holidays, spring allergies, and summer move outs. (Many of the customers were renters or college students who needed to have their place professionally cleaned as part of their lease agreement.)

We also included information that people may not know, such as the fact that Flatirons Carpet and Hardwood is environmentally-friendly and uses products that can help relieve allergies. We produced a short video that was humorous and linked to it from the email newsletters, as well as to videos of impressive new equipment that they got.

The results were astounding, as Becky testified:

"Email marketing helps remind our customers of all the services we do. We usually get four to five jobs within the first 10 hours of sending out our newsletter."

Becky Shultz
Flatiron Carpet & Hardwood

How much business are you leaving on the table by not staying in touch with your customers via email marketing? How many of them totally forget who you are, what you do, or even how to contact you? If quarterly email newsletters can drum up this much business for a carpet cleaning company, imagine what it could do for you if you communicated with greater frequency.

Stand Out in Noisy Email Inboxes with Professional Design

I read recently that the average person receives more than 150 emails a day. People typically have a work email and multiple personal email addresses. Everyone, it seems, is trying to send them junk. As such, it is more important than ever that your email communication is professional, concise, recognizable, and adds value to the person receiving it. Otherwise, you'll end up in the spam folder.

Chances are, someone is opening your email on their smartphone while they are doing something else. Maybe they're waiting for food to warm up in the microwave, or they are in line at the grocery store. If the person is opening the message on her mobile device, she will make a decision instantly, based on the sender address or subject line, whether to continue reading or mark it as spam. That's why it is important that your email newsletter design matches the branding of everything else in your business.

Too often, I see businesses with really chintzy-looking generic templates that haven't been customized with the colors, fonts, the logo, or other imagery from their business.

At a minimum, your email campaigns should include:

- **A recognizable sender name.** Do customers recognize "Bob Johnson" (the owner's name), or would they more immediately recognize "Main Street BBQ?" It can vary per business, but make sure that the emails are being sent from a name that is recognizable so people know who and why you are emailing them.

- **An email address hosted at your domain.** Dude, you don't work for comcast.net or yahoo.com and you definitely don't work for MSN! (If you work at aol.com, get out. Go home. That's just weird.) If you're a legitimate business and you want people to take you seriously, get professional email hosting ending in your domain name (yourbusinessname.com).

- **Your logo, colors, font, and other visual branding elements used in your marketing** reinforce your branding with your logo so people know who you are right away.

- **Your headshot.** If you are a real estate agent or salesperson, your email should include your headshot so people recognize you.

- **Contact info.** Your business phone, email, website, address and a link to Google Maps, if you're a brick-and-mortar location.

Five Commandments for Better Results from Email Campaigns

These aren't just tips. They are commandments. Do these five things with each email campaign... or your email won't even get opened or even make it into the inbox.

1. Write Strong Subject Lines That People Actually Want To Open

No one cares about you or your "September Newsletter." If you want people to actually open your email, write subject lines that answer the question, "What's in it for me?" Keep the subject line at less than eight words and be sure to see how it displays on mobile. Do you get the benefit of opening the email across succinctly?

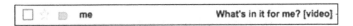

Your subject line = What's in it for me?

All of your marketing (all of it) needs to answer the question, "What's in it for me?" Who cares about you and your special and your "newsletter?" No one cares about that. Your subject line is your chance to get people to open your email.

Examples of Good, Bad, and Ugly Subject Lines

Here are a couple examples of good email subject lines, some bad, and some downright ugly!

Nonprofit

Bad example:

> *"Subject: March newsletter*
>
> *Hey I just wanted to send you my March newsletter. I don't know if you should really open it. You could. We have some specials and we'll send it again next month, same thing probably."*

Using a subject line like "March newsletter" is pathetic. Don't do this. Nobody cares about March newsletter.

Good example:

> *"Subject: Tomorrow: Need three hammers. Can you help?*
>
> *One of my local nonprofits needs help. Can I help? Why, yes, I can. I'm going to open the email and find out exactly how."*

Pet Store

Bad example: *"Joe's Pet Store newsletter."*

> *"Subject: Joe's Pet Store newsletter"*

Good example: "Alert: Help your dog beat the heat."

"Subject: Alert: Help your dog beat the heat

I can help Ralph my dog, beat the heat."

Children's Dance Classes

Bad example:

"Children's classes."

They totally forgot who's sending this. It's probably from, like, Mary Sanchez. But who is Mary Sanchez with children's classes?

Good example:

"Still time. Openings available for children's classes!"

You get the idea. If you want people to open the message, put some life into your subject lines. Keep it less than eight words and remember:

"What's in it for me?"

2. Format for Mobile

More than 50% of email is opened on smartphones — and that will likely continue to increase. Even though many business owners check email on their phone, they don't think to preview their campaigns on mobile. As a result, they send out big, floppy, gigantic email campaigns that look awful on mobile — and cut their open rates and conversions by half!

Here are a few best practices for mobile:

Use a responsive one-column layout

Sorry, it's not 2009 anymore. It's time to ditch the two-column layout. I know that side bar was so wonderful for including inspiring quotes, links to additional content, and other junk — but it looks awful on mobile. If you use MailChimp, Constant Contact, HubSpot, or another email marketing service provider, choose a template suited for mobile devices.

I searched my email history and dug up this gem from 2010 — just before I switched to using a one-column layout. Below is a screenshot of the email when I open it on my iPhone using the Gmail app. See how this two column layout is barely legible?

●●●●● AT&T M-Cell 🤖   **11:09 AM**   72% 🔋

‹   📥   🗑   ✉   •••

From: **Jack Jostes** <Jack@ramblinjackson.com>
Date: Wed, May 26, 2010 at 7:11 AM
Subject: How to master Social Media, S.E.O, and Web Content
To: jackjostes@gmail.com

Having trouble viewing this email? Please click here   Write a review / Forward to a Friend
To ensure delivery, please add Jack@RamblinJackson.com to your address book.   SmartUnsubscribe℠

Dear Coloradans, Countrymen, and do-it-yourself folks,

I'm excited to announce my upcoming workshop,
Sink or Swim -- How to Master Social Media, Search Engine Optimization, and Web Content,

Andrea Vahl, Reid Peterson & I will break down complex Internet marketing techniques into simple, tangible, & immediately applicable strategies that will help businesses increase web-driven sales.

Please check out our video and flier, and forward this to anyone who would benefit from improving their business's web presence.

Looking Forward,

Jack Jostes

A success story:

"Jack rewrote the text on four pages of our website, making them more concise, more readable and including better calls to action. The bounce rate on our home page has gone down by nearly 10%, showing that the text on our website is more inviting and resulting in higher click-through rates on our website. I'm not certain what more I can say that than I am DEFINITELY planning on hiring Jack again in the future and would recommend his services to anyone looking to enhance their marketing content."

-Nathan Jansch
Owner, The Boardroom Executive Suites

Sink_Or_Swim_Video

3. Include Strong Calls to Action That Make the Next Step Easy

What do you want people to *do*? Make it easy for them to take the next step — book an appointment, register online, or accomplish whatever your goal of the email is — with strong calls to action.

VISIT OUR WEBSITE

4. List Segmentation: Send the Right Message to the Right Market

Look at this email I got from the department store Dillard's. It's for some cosmetic product women apparently put on their eyeballs and mom jeans. I bought one thing from them. One thing. A *men's* suit. From the *men's* department. #socialmediafail

Make sure the right people get the right message.

5. Link to Content on Your Website

Because most people open emails on their smartphone, they're definitely not going to read all of your content in their inbox. Give people a taste of "what's in it for me" and then link to longer content, such as blog posts or videos, on your website.

Email Tip: Using video in email massively increases your click-thru and open rates. The best way to do this is to take a screenshot of your video with the play button in the image and link to its location on your website. I'd recommend NOT linking people directly to YouTube*, because you'd have better control over what they see and what they click on next if they were on your own website.

*I respect the idea that driving people to YouTube increases your YouTube view count, which increases the likelihood of people finding your business on YouTube — but for most *local businesses,* I'd recommend directing people to a page on your own website with the video embedded.

Get the latest digital marketing trends to
Get FOUND Online by your best customers
delivered to your inbox every Friday!
Sign up for my free weekly video series,
Friday's Ramblin Roundup, at
ramblinjackson.com/roundup

Generating Results with Strong Offers

You should create email marketing campaigns with a clear, specific, and measurable outcome in mind.

If your goal is to get people to buy something, present them with a strong offer that incites them to take action by a certain date.

What you offer people should vary depending on where they are in their customer journey and customer lifecycle with your business.

For customers who haven't bought in a while, consider a reactivation campaign containing an offer that welcomes them back. This can be particularly effective for a yoga studio, for example, whose customer hasn't been to class in a while. Bring them back with an offer they can't refuse!

New Customer Welcome

You could also use email marketing as a New Customer Welcome campaign or series, to send customers on-boarding information and helpful tips about how to work with your company, use your products, engage with your social media, and so on.

One of my clients owns both a landscaping company and garden center. While each business has its own unique clientbase, there is great opportunity to upsell by making an offer via email.

That could come in the form of a coupon, special deal, registration link for an event, or a link to a video and landing page where they can learn more and take action.

Here's an example of a welcome series for a Pilates studio:

Celebrate Birthdays and Anniversaries

A great reactivation campaign for retail businesses is to celebrate birthdays and anniversaries. If your customers aren't comfortable giving their full birthdate, you could still likely get their birthday month and send them a coupon or another offer.

This is an example of a campaign we ran for Frame
It, a custom frame shop in Littleton, Colorado.
Frame It has been in business for more than 37
years and their customers love the owner, Nancy
Hallowell.

We ran a specific offer: $99 framing special ($225 value) for three days — Thursday through Saturday. The email went out on Thursday at 6 a.m. and generated 25 repeat purchases.

The email included a holiday photo of Nancy in the shop surrounded by some of the holiday gifts she sold there, clearly described the offer, and contained important details, such as store hours, address, phone number, and a link to Google Maps, which five people clicked on mobile (20% of the people who redeemed the offer).

The campaign had a good response because:

- The offer was set to a limited time period that created urgency;

- The subject line, copy, and imagery were clear and concise.

Collecting Email Addresses to Grow Your List

To do email marketing, you need to have email addresses! Since many business people have a laser focus on acquiring new customers, they can overlook their existing customer base. While getting new email addresses is a good idea, start with your existing customers.

Here are a few ways to get email addresses from your existing customers:

1. Export from your bookkeeping program;

2. Website contact form submissions;

WordPress Tip: Easily integrate your email marketing program with your WordPress website contact form using Gravity Forms.

3. One-on-one client emails;

4. Ask them in person or on the telephone ("Bob, would you like us to send you our guide, How to Buy the Perfect Engagement Ring?");

5. Give away free cake!

Portillo's Hot Dogs is an iconic Chicago chain that serves some of the world's best hot dogs, Italian beef sandwiches, char-grilled burgers, and fresh salads.

In 2015, to celebrate their 52nd birthday, they started a customer appreciation program: the Portillo's Birthday Club. Members can get a free slice of chocolate cake on their birthday. To become a Portillo's Birthday Club member, all you have to do is sign up at www.portillos.com/freecake/.

They market this free cake club on their website, through social media, and on branded cups in the store.

The program is brilliant, for three reasons:

1. By collecting your email address, mailing address, and birthday, they can now continue marketing to you via email and direct mail with offers that will make you more likely to buy from them;

2. They have your birthdate and can make you feel special;

3. **It's awesome. Who doesn't want free cake?!** (And who celebrates their 52nd birthday?!)

Frequency: How Often Should You Send?

I recommend that you send your email newsletter <u>as regularly as you can provide value</u>. At Ramblin

Jackson, we send out Friday's Ramblin Roundup every week — and our clients love it.

We regularly get feedback *from people who spend money with us* because the emails we send add value. In the digital marketing industry, there is something new every week and we can provide value by keeping them up to date in an informative and entertaining way.

If you can't commit to weekly, at least do monthly. Quarterly is OK... but three months is a long time to go by, and someone could easily forget all about you during that time.

What Day and Time Should You Send?

Many people ask when they should send their newsletter. The answer: it depends on your market.

Whatever timeframe you choose, follow through on the expectation you set when people sign up. If you tell people they'll get a quarterly newsletter, send it quarterly... not monthly or weekly or daily.

The #1 reason people unsubscribe
from email marketing lists is
because they get too much email.

Constant Contact customers see good open rates Tuesday, Wednesday, and Thursday mornings at about 9 a.m., however, HubSpot's Science Of Email Report[4] shows that Tuesdays are actually the worst! I've also seen some people send on the weekend. A lot of retail businesses might see a high open rate on the weekend when people are shopping.

The way that I would go about it is to test your list and *find out what works best for your business*. Experiment. Send some emails at a certain time of day for a few weeks or months, then try a different time and day with a different list. Compare the open rates to see which work best.

Also, frankly, if you're new to email marketing and not sending regularly — don't get too hung up on the day of the week. Just get it out already.

Selecting the Right Email Marketing Software for Your Business

Email should become a core part of your business marketing and communication, so be sure to choose the best solution for your business needs. You'll use email marketing software to manage your contacts and database, design and send email campaigns, monitor results and analytics, keep in touch with existing clients, and add on new clients.

Why You Need Email Marketing Software and the Problem with Sending from Gmail.

Many people do not realize that using a personal email account — such as Gmail, Comcast, AOL, Yahoo, or even a professionally-hosted email account — to send out mass marketing emails is a) against the CAN-SPAM Act and b) totally ineffective.

The CAN-SPAM Act

The CAN-SPAM Act, signed by President Bush in 2003, is aimed at protecting people from spam. The acronym CAN-SPAM derives from the bill's full name: Controlling the Assault of Non-Solicited Pornography And Marketing Act of 2003.

To make your marketing emails compliant with the CAN-SPAM Act, you need to include your physical address along with a link that people can click to remove themselves from your list There are other requirements but those are the two most important. They are definitely not an option when you send a ton of emails from your personal account.

Also, after you add eight people to an email, the changes that your personal email program will send the message to all of them decreases significantly.

Pet peeve: Being cc'd on a marketing email (from someone I hardly know) to a bunch of people I don't know… and then those people add my email address to their spammy list.

No branding control

When you send mass emails from your personal account, you have no control over how the message will appear when people receive it. You can't customize your colors and fonts or even add your logo.

No analytics

Did anyone actually receive the emails? Did they open them? Did they click on them? With a personal email account, you have no analytics to measure the performance of your campaigns.

Poor list segmentation

Another disadvantage of using a personal email account to send email marketing campaigns is a lack of list segmentation. Remember how I received the mom jeans email from Dillard's after buying a men's suit? Don't do that. Ideally, you'd send targeted communications to different lists of people based on demographic, psychographic, and customer lifecycle stages. Your personal email account makes segmentation almost impossible.

Five Factors to Consider
When Selecting Your
Email Marketing Software

There are tons of email marketing software providers out there. And, as with most things, you get what you pay for. Here are five factors to consider when selecting your email marketing software.

1. Deliverability

The deliverability rate is the number of emails that actually *get into the person's email inbox.* There are skeezy 100% free email software companies that have a very low deliverability rate, which means fewer people will receive your marketing message.

A good deliverability rate to look for is above 97%. That means that 97 out of the 100 (valid) email addresses in your database receive the email. Cheap or free email companies, or ones with very low quality standards, will likely allow spammy marketers to use their program. That can get their servers flagged, which means fewer of your list members will get your message.

2. Integration

Does (or should) your email program need to integrate with your point of sale, CRM, website shopping cart, online scheduling program, or other business software?

Make a list of what your email marketing program actually needs to accomplish, which software you use on a daily or monthly basis, and then see if the companies you're considering integrate with it.

Wouldn't it be great if you could *automatically* email customers who haven't been to your store in a while? With the right integration to your CRM, that could happen.

3. Customer Support

Does the email software vendor answer the telephone, provide live chat, or respond to emails? Or, does customer support only consist of it self-guided tutorials on their website?

The access to prompt customer support is a major consideration for me when purchasing software for my business *because I need to protect my most valuable asset: my TIME.*

How much is your time worth? How much time (and money) could you save by buying software from a company that costs a little bit more but has superior customer support that could take care of issues for you faster, better, and with less stress?

If you make a $50,000 per year salary, that equates to about $24.04 an hour based on a 40-hour work week. But let's be honest: You're probably a small business owner working way more than forty hours a week. (Hopefully, you can grow your business to the point where you're making much more than

$50K a year working less than or close to 40 hours a week, but let's run with this $50K salary example for now.)

If you have a "free" email software program, but it takes you even one hour longer per month (let alone per week) than a $20 per month service that has prompt support to get your email campaigns completed (because you're digging around on a website watching self-guided videos, etc.) — you *are* paying more! And you could likely spend that hour on other revenue-generating activities.

The value of customer support is saved time and money

MailChimp is free for under 2,000 list members... but includes NO customer support, with the exception of some links to tutorials on their website. If you're like many of my clients, you're very busy and your time is extremely valuable. If you make more than $50,000 a year, it may be worth it to pay a company like Constant Contact to have access to a support person who can solve your problem in 20 minutes versus spending three hours trying to research and do it yourself using a "free" program.

4. Ease of Use

This consideration is similar to the support one in the amount of time it can save you. Choose a software platform that is relatively easy to use so you spend as little time as possible.

Related: Access to vendors who know the software.

There is also value in choosing software that is widely used in the marketing industry. This will increase the likelihood that you'd find a marketing vendor or company who can work with your program should you choose to hire it out.

5. Analytics

Select an email marketing software vendor that has, at minimum, open rates, click thru rates, and bounces as part of its analytics. Your program should also integrate with Google Analytics so you can see which campaigns are generating website visitors — particularly those who are active on your website, scheduling appointments, filling out your contact form, etc.

Key Takeaways From Drive Repeat Business With Email Marketing

- Repeat customers will spend a lot with you. Keep in touch with your customers via email.

- Use professional email marketing software, not your personal email account.

- Segment your lists based on relevant geographic, psychographic, demographic, and customer lifecycle stage information.

- Focus on growing your email list. Ask every prospect you talk with to join your email marketing program.

- Consider the value of your time and the true cost of "free" when selecting your email program.

- Think of the Lifetime Value of your best customers, and be sure to focus some of your marketing efforts on retention and upsells.

9

LEVERAGE SOCIAL MEDIA MARKETING TO ENGAGE AND CONVERT

"Content is fire; social media is gasoline."

- Jay Baer

As a small business owner, when you hear about "social media," you may get overwhelmed thinking you need to be on all of the newest and most popular social networks. But don't worry; you don't.

While you don't have to be everywhere, you should be visible and active on at least two of the social networks where your customers are present. It's much better to have an active social media profile on two social networks that get results than to have a partially-active profile on ten networks that generate no results.

This chapter will help you figure out which social networks to use, how to post great content, and how to generate leads with Facebook advertising.

Share Your Business Experience Using Social Media

One of the greatest aspects of social media is that you can give people a little taste of the experience of working with your business. Best of all, you can create a lot of this content just by using a smartphone.

Document, Don't Create

Many people get bogged down with the time it takes to create content for social media. An approach I like that is especially relevant to personal branding for CEOs, business leaders, and public speakers is the one taken by Gary Vaynerchuk, a well-known internet marketing personality and author of several books on the topic of social media including one of my favorites, *Crush It!: Why NOW Is the Time to Cash In on Your Passion.*[1]

The approach: "Document, Don't Create." Vaynerchuk takes his fans and followers behind the scenes of what he's doing on a day-to-day basis through a photo or quick video on Facebook and Instagram. From his perspective, this can be a great way to attract new customers and give people a glimpse into what life is like as a small business owner.

7 Social Media Post Ideas + Real Local Business Examples

1. **Behind the scenes** - If you're a seafood restaurant like Wild Standard in Boulder, which serves big beautiful salmon, record a short Facebook Live video to share the excitement!

2. **Success stories** - Everyone loves success stories. Maybe you're the owner of a Pilates studio that helped someone regain their shoulder movement and prevent surgery. Take a photo or video of that person and share the story on Instagram and Facebook.

3. **New product photos** - Did you get a new
   shipment of scarves at your gift shop? Have
   your staff pose for a fun photo to showcase
   them.

4. **Employee highlights** - Take a photo of a staff member on their birthday or when they accomplish something cool. Everyone loves a little acknowledgement!

5. **Upcoming classes** - Do you have an upcoming class or event? Record a quick Facebook Live video to let people know what it's about.

6. **Share a Taste of the Experience!** - If you have a restaurant, this is a no-brainer. Make people hungry!

Tiramisu, a popular coffee-flavoured italian custard dessert. Coffee lovers rejoice! **#Coffee #**... See More

7. **A link to a helpful blog post on your website** - Distribute frequently-updated website content such as blog posts to social networks. Put the content out there where people can find it more easily.

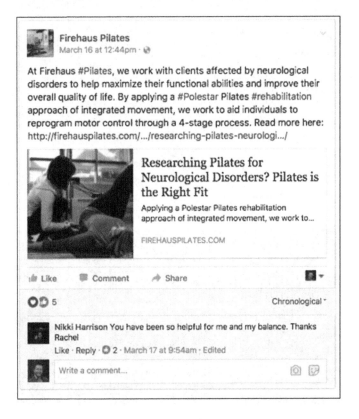

Notice how a client of Firehaus Pilates commented, "You have been so helpful for me and my balance. Thanks Rachel."

THAT is word of mouth.
THAT is social proof.
You can't pay for that!

(Well, you may need to pay someone to make the posts but that's another matter.)

A prospective customer might check out their Facebook page, read the post, and that testimonial could help seal the deal. This is just one example of how posting content and engaging your existing customers can lead to new business and referrals.

What rich insight you have into the experience of those businesses I just shared! _That_ is the power of great photography and social media. While some of those were taken by professional photographers, I believe you can do a lot with just your smartphone.

Use Hashtags That Customers in Your Geographic Market Use

A hashtag is defined as a word or phrase preceded by a hash or pound sign (#) and used to identify messages on a specific topic. (More experienced business people may remember these as the pound sign.) It's a technique used often on social networks like Instagram and Twitter.

Using the right hashtags can help more people see your posts and discover your business.

Social Media Tip: Use Geographic Hashtags. While it's likely that a bunch of people are geeking out about something in your industry using a certain hashtag, remember that the purpose of your marketing to is attract local customers to your local business. As such, it's wise to use geographic hashtags for your city, county, and state (e.g.,. #Boulder #Colorado).

For example, people who are looking at the hashtag #Boulder will see my posts and, chances are, they are in Boulder or planning to go there.

While there are hashtag finding tools out there, don't overthink it. Just use Instagram on your smartphone as a starting point. (You can also research this from your desktop browser at

Instagram.com and you don't need to be logged in when searching.)

See how many more posts there are for #Boulder vs. #BoulderCO? We're on the right track.

Here's an example of a local frame shop (who is also my client) that popped up when I looked at the hashtag #boulder on Instagram.

boulderframes Unique typography design, called for a clean and contemporary custom frame design...love the way this turned out! @thecalmgallery
#boulder #frames #boulderframes #typography
www.boulderfastframe.com

Social Media Tip: Save a list of hashtags in a note on your phone. When it comes time to make a post, you can quickly copy and paste the hashtags in.

Be Careful and Research Each Hashtag

Once you start looking around, you'll find out what hashtags are popular in your industry and your local market. Before you start using them, make sure to test them first.

One time, one of my employees started using #FRR as an abbreviation for our weekly video series, Friday's Ramblin Roundup. When we clicked on the hashtag after the post went live we found some posts... with which we didn't want to be associated. You can check that one out on your own, but take my advice — do your research first before arbitrarily adding a tag!

Keep Content Fresh with a Blog

If your website is built through wordpress.org or many other popular content management systems, you may have the opportunity to publish blog posts. I recommend this approach: Post from your main domain rather than creating a separate blog site using a platform such as wordpress.com, Blogspot, or Typepad. (See more information about this in the chapter on web design.)

Site Freshness

Site freshness refers to how "fresh" or current the content is on a website. According to study published on the Moz blog by SEO expert Cyrus Shepard, "10 Illustrations Of How Fresh Content

May Influence Google Rankings,"[2] one of the
benefits of blogging *with quality content that real
humans would like to read* is called Site Freshness.

This means that if you're in a really competitive
market and your competitors have equally
excellent websites, strong SEO, good reviews, etc.
— site freshness could be a differentiating factor
that may help Google rank your website over
theirs.

> Key point: Write quality content
> that humans want to read.

I am by no means suggesting that if you churn out
low quality blog posts every day that it will have
any positive impact on your rankings or business
whatsoever. You need to write good content that
people want to read and share online. Google is
increasingly improving their algorithm to consider
the *quality* of content, partly through engagement
metrics such as how long people spend on a
webpage, how many other pages link to it, etc.

Internal Linking

Another benefit of publishing blog posts on your
website is the opportunity to add links from the
posts to the other pages of your site. This is called
internal linking.

Remember, <u>Google ranks web pages, not websites,</u> and building links to individual pages can help them rank in search results. For example, if you were a dentist in Austin, Texas, who wrote a blog post about "The Top 3 Foods That Stain Your Teeth," it would make sense to link to the Teeth Whitening services page on your site.

This will not only help readers of the blog post learn more about your teeth whitening services but would also help the teeth whitening services page show up in searches on Google for "teeth whitening austin tx". Of course, as with any SEO tactic, you need to be careful not to overdo this or do it in a spammy way.

SEO Tip: Check out the Yoast SEO Premium plugin feature for Internal Linking on WordPress sites. This plugin will read the content of your website to help you find other pages that may be worth linking to.

Ideas for Local Business Blog Posts

Answer FAQs on Your Website

Chance are, if people are asking your business questions offline, they're probably also googling them. Publishing FAQs as blog posts is a great SEO idea that can also make for helpful social media content. When people are researching a purchasing decision, getting answers to their questions from YOUR website helps position you as an expert from which they'll want to buy.

Another benefit of FAQ style content is ranking in Google's Answer Box search results.

An example of the search results for "How many hours do you need to get your license in Colorado?" brings about this FAQ style result from a private business, Colorado Driving Institute.

> How many hours do you need to get your license in Colorado?   ^
>
> Effective April 23, **2007 - 6 hours** of Behind-the-Wheel Lessons before Drive Test:
> You are required to hold your first instruction permit for at least twelve months and
> be at least **16** years of age before you can get a driver's license in Colorado.
>
> Colorado: New Driving Laws... - Colorado Driving Institute
> coloradodrivinginstitute.com/new-laws.html
>
> Search for: How many hours do you need to get your license in Colorado?

What kind of questions do your prospective clients, patients, and customers have that you could answer?

Copywriting Brainstorm Tip: Ask your salespeople, servers, office managers, and those in contact with customers on a day to day business, "What questions do you find our customers asking you on a daily basis?" Also, look at Google related search results.

Searches related to how many hours do you need to get your driver's license colorado

colorado **drivers** license **requirements for minors**

driver license colorado **appointment**

colorado **learner's permit rules over 18**

getting a colorado driver's license **from out of state**

colorado **drivers** license **requirements over 18**

how to **prove residency in** colorado

colorado **drivers** license **test**

minor learners permit colorado

Recap a Conference You Attended and Relay the Takeaways to Your Customers

If you attend an industry conference or tradeshow, summarize your key takeaways in a blog post to share with your team, clients, and industry.

When I attend conferences, I always do a roundup video + blog post with my key takeaways. This lets my customers know that I am out and active in the industry, staying abreast of trends to keep their businesses competitive.

Also, I optimize my posts so that when people in my industry search for information about a conference, they may find my site. Being visible to the folks searching these queries may be helpful to recruiting.

MozCon Local 2017 Takeaways For Small Business - Ramblin Jackson
www.ramblinjackson.com/2017/03/17/mozcon-local-2017-takeaways/ ▾
5 days ago - Check out our recap of 2017 MozCon Local conference to see my key takeaways about
what you need to know about local SEO to keep your ...

Searches related to mozcon local

moz conference seattle	search marketing expo
moz conference 2017	moz seattle layoffs
seo conferences 2017	smx advanced
moz 2017	smx advanced 2017

After the Sale Resources

In addition to helping you acquire new customers, blog posts can serve a great operational purpose for your business after the sale.

Similar to the FAQs, what questions do people have *after* they buy from you? How can you add value after the sale so they utilize your product or service effectively, remember you, and refer you?

The great thing about this approach is that you can automate this follow up using an email marketing autoresponder sequence. Create the content as blog posts on your website, then craft a series of emails that you send to your clients automatically. This can also be an effective way to automate a survey or review request.

Ideas for Post-Sale Content

- How-to content

- Related products and services

- Fun photos of clients using the product or service

- Tutorial videos

Stop Lollygagging
You Have to Pay to Play

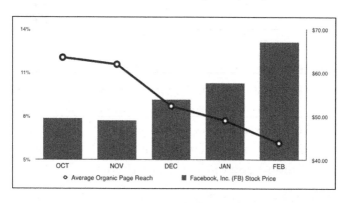

Here's a nice graphic from marketing strategist and author Jay Baer showing how, as Facebook's stock price increased, average organic page reach declined. (Organic reach is the number of people who see your posts without you having to pay for results.)

The PR firm Ogilvy & Mather visualizes it nicely here as well:

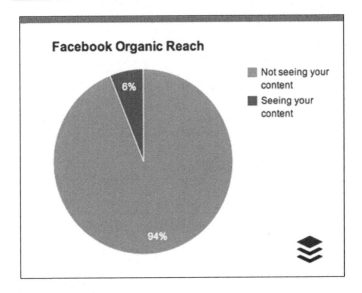

Just because you're posting and have Likes doesn't mean anyone is seeing it — except for maybe your mom. I love it when my mom comments on my Facebook posts. She is such a wonderful woman and probably one of just five people who see the posts when I don't pay to boost them.

This doesn't necessarily mean that organic reach is dead, but if you have zero followers it likely does.

Why Facebook Advertising is Currently the Greatest Promotional Opportunity for Small Business

Facebook isn't just a social network; it's an advertising company. Not only is it the largest social network on the planet with nearly two billion users at last count, it is an advertising company that rakes in billions each year from sponsored content.

As far as paid advertising goes, I believe Facebook Advertising is the greatest opportunity for small businesses, chiefly because of the amount of data Facebook can target through its advertising.

Important note about Facebook advertising following election scandals, etc.

In the spring of 2018, Facebook testified before the United States Senate over data leaks, the sharing of fake news in its newsfeed, and hate speech in its program.

During the 2016 U.S. presidential election, a U.K. academic named Aleksandr Kogan created a quiz on Facebook and wrongly sold the data of 50 million Facebook users to Cambridge Analytica, a political and data mining company that allegedly used the information in Donald Trump's election campaign. Facebook CEO Mark Zuckerberg apologized. "We didn't take a broad enough view of our responsibility, and that was a big mistake," Zuckerberg said. "It was my mistake, and I'm sorry."

I agree, Facebook could have done a better job protecting its users' data. It was also clear in the hearing that the Senate has little understanding of how the internet actually works and that *people choose to use Facebook and choose to agree to Facebook's terms of service.*

I personally still advocate using Facebook and Facebook Advertising for small businesses, but I do think you need to be careful with what information you put online about yourself and your business.

Additionally, what I'm advocating below is that you **work within Facebook's Guidelines, the General Data Protection Regulation (GDPR) , as well as your local, state, and federal guidelines regarding personal data.**

**Three things you can do if you
don't like Facebook's use of your
personal data in advertising**

1.   Don't use Facebook.

2.   Don't share personal information on Facebook or other internet sites that you don't want advertisers to see. Update your settings at facebook.com/privacy/

3.   Stop whining. Use a different website. Do something else.

If you disagree with Facebook's ad platform and use of data, that's OK. Reading what follows will at least help you understand how it all works (and maybe make you change your privacy settings.)

Facebook's Data Centric Partners Know What You Like

While many know that Facebook can target their demographic information (age, sex, location, marital status, education, and more), and that it can target the things you do while you're using Facebook (posts you like, pages you follow, and so on), many people are surprised by how much *offline* data Facebook has about them.

Facebook has partnerships with data capture companies such as Datalogic, Epsilon, Bluekai, and

Axciom. These companies gather reams of data from the Census Bureau, insurance companies, credit card companies, and the like and package it up to Facebook, which then resells it to businesses for advertising targeting.

Things you could target with Facebook:

- **Life events** - engagements, marriages, divorces, births, and deaths

- **Recent purchases** - cars, clothing, a home, and type of groceries

- **Financial activities** - banking, investments, loans, and debts

- **Automotive** - what car you have, your boat, or motorcycle

- **Travel** - where you've traveled to recently

- **Residential data** - renter or homeowner.

- **Connections** - bands and artists you like, politicians you support, and brands you follow

If you want to target a 42-year-old woman in Boulder who drives a Subaru and likes Golden Retrievers and recently traveled to Europe and does yoga... you could.

Not that that would be hard in Boulder anyways, but you get the idea. What kind of life events would make someone an ideal fit for your business? You can target them on Facebook with your ads.

Facebook Custom Audiences

Facebook Advertising has a feature called Custom Audiences where you can upload existing contact data that you already have, including email addresses, phone numbers, and website visitors. That means if you upload your database of customer email addresses and Facebook has those same addresses associated with Facebook Profiles, you can advertise to those people or even exclude them from seeing advertising.

1. Email Addresses

First, there's email addresses. You can get a list of your customers email addresses by exporting your Quickbooks' contacts, your Constant Contact or another email newsletter contact list, or your sales CRM. Chances are, you have tons of email addresses, and if you don't, you should start collecting them!

Facebook Advertising Tip: Look at the top 20% of your customers and create a Lookalike Audience.

You could also use email addresses to create what Facebook refers to as a "Lookalike" audience. It works much the same way as Custom Audiences; just upload your customer contact list(s) and Facebook will match them to others who share similar characteristics.

2. Phone Numbers

Remember that time Facebook asked to help "Secure your account" by entering in your mobile phone number? That's one way it have may gotten your digits. Otherwise, many people just add their phone number to their profile. Similar to uploading email addresses, you can upload a sheet of mobile phone numbers as a Custom Audience.

3. Website Visitors

Have you ever looked at a product on Amazon or another ecommerce site (or any site for that matter) and then saw it again when you were on Facebook? That's called "retargeting." Here's how it works:

You (or a web developer) install a Facebook "Pixel," a tracking code to the HTML of your website that detects when a Facebook user pays a visit.

```
<!-- Facebook Pixel Code -->
<script>
!function(f,b,e,v,n,t,s){if(f.fbq)return;n=f.fbq=function(){n.callMethod?
n.callMethod.apply(n,arguments):n.queue.push(arguments)};if(!f._fbq)f._fbq=n;
n.push=n;n.loaded=!0;n.version='2.0';n.queue=[];t=b.createElement(e);t.async=!0;
t.src=v;s=b.getElementsByTagName(e)[0];s.parentNode.insertBefore(t,s)}(window,
document,'script','//connect.facebook.net/en_US/fbevents.js');

fbq('init', '1234567890');
fbq('track', 'PageView');

</script>
<noscript><img height="1" width="1" style="display:none"
src="https://www.facebook.com/tr?id=1234567890&ev=PageView&noscript=1"
/></noscript>
<!-- End Facebook Pixel Code -->
```
Facebook pixel

When Facebook "sees" the pixel, it knows to show the person your ads. It's a way to help them remember you and, hopefully, take action. (Using a Facebook Pixel with retargeting is also a great way to leverage other marketing efforts, such as SEO, email marketing, or other form of advertising.)

———————— ————————

Facebook Advertising Tip: Track people who have visited specific pages of your site.

One of the coolest parts about Facebook retargeting is that you can show people who have visited a particular page of your website ads specific to the page. This is especially useful for ecommerce sites but works with any site.

For example, if you run a Pilates studio offering Pilates for seniors and someone checked out that page on your site, you could retarget them with ads that include testimonials from seniors, blog posts about Pilates for seniors, and special offers to join the next class.

Maybe you're a recreation center owner. Someone visiting the swimming pool page can see retargeting ads with the schedule for your master's team.

If you own a custom jewelry shop, you could retarget people who have visited the engagement rings gallery using photos or blog posts about inspiring engagement stories, and then make an offer.

Effective Facebook Ad Types for Local Businesses

Carousel Ads

Carousel Ads are great for visual content. This ad format consists of a series of photos that can end with a link to a web page or a contact form directly in Facebook.

Jasper's Market
Sponsored · ✍

Jasper's is more than just groceries! You can now find all of your cooking tools and utensils on our website.

Set of five white ceramic bowls

White ceramic mortar and pes'

$20

$25

18 Reactions 3 Comments 1 Share

👍 Like   💬 Comment   ↪ Share

Facebook Video Ads

One of my favorite types of advertising are Facebook Video ads. You can create ads — often without sound, since many people scroll through Facebook on their smartphone without the sound turned on — that contain beautiful imagery and attractively-formatted text to convey your message. A 20-to-30-second video can grab people's attention, and the right call to action can inspire them to do business with you.

Lead Generation Ads

A lead generation ad could be a Facebook Video or Carousel ad, or just a straight image ad, that concludes with a call to action requesting a prospect's contact information. In general, the more contact information you request in a form, the fewer people will complete it (but you'll likely get a higher quality of lead).

A lead generation ad could collect a person's information in exchange for access to a downloadable PDF, coupon, or request a follow-up from the business just like a website contact form.

We have successfully run lead generation campaigns for all kinds of businesses, from retailers offering coupons all the way up to dentists promoting first-time visits to landscapers booking appointments for $50,000+ landscape installations, and even a private golf club whose lifetime customer value is north of $30,000.

Using Facebook for Job Recruiting

Facebook Advertising can be used for other things besides acquiring new customers. For instance, ProMaster Handyman and Home Repair of Cincinnati uses Facebook ads to recruit employees for his home repair and handyman installation company.

Creating Direct Response
Offers That Generate Results

While Facebook's Advertising targeting capabilities are pretty great, what really matters is that you are marketing *an offer that your target market will respond to.* "Brand awareness" should never be the goal of small business ad campaigns but a by-product. In other words, you should use advertising to get customers, not generate "awareness."

Most ads just plain suck because they lack two components of effective direct response marketing: urgency and scarcity.

If there's no urgency, why would they act now instead of later or not at all? If there is an overabundance, why act now when the customer can get it later.

Here's an example of a very effective direct response social media ad campaign we ran for a local dentist.

> Book your $99 New Patient Special
> Before April 1st and
> Get a Free Electric Toothbrush*
> *Limited to first 30 patients.

This type of offer is a gift with purchase. It is effective because it has:

- A specific deadline

- An offer (free toothbrush) when you book your appointment

- Scarcity — only 30 available

How much will you pay to acquire a new customer? How can you offer something that gets them to take action?

Recommended reading: *No B.S. Guide To Social Media Marketing* by Dan Kennedy and Kim Walsh Phillips.[3]

Funnel Them into Leads with Landing Pages and Automation

If your ads don't include a specific offer that people redeem (like a coupon or a special or something), they could be lead-generation focused. Lead generation ads are where you'll offer up a valuable piece of content or information that a prospective client would receive in exchange for giving you his contact info.

If your customers have a longer buying cycle that may require research, it could be a good idea to warm them up with a marketing campaign consisting of videos, blog posts, webinars, and other content that helps educate them and establishes your brand as an authority. The best part about this model is that you can leverage marketing automation software to have a lot of this activity occur automatically after you set it up.

> Offer a piece of content that answers a specific problem or pain point of your customers, such as a guide, checklist, or video series.

Create a Landing Page Where People Need to Opt in

Direct Facebook users to a landing page on your website that describes the offer and then funnels them into giving you their email or contact info. An important distinction between landing pages and regular web pages is that landing pages *are designed to convert people to one specific outcome, such as a contact form completion.*

There are a lot of tools to use to build landing pages but the one I like best is LeadPages.net. It has a great many templates that make setting up landing pages an easy process.

Key Takeaways From Leverage Social Media Marketing To Engage And Convert

- Use photos and videos to take fans and followers behind the scenes to show what your business is like.

- Use relevant hashtags but research them first; save them to your phone for quick access.

- Add a blog to keep content fresh and distribute posts to social networks.

- Make Facebook advertising a go-to tactic.

- Have the entire sales funnel planned out with a direct-response campaign before you begin advertising.

- Use Facebook ads to convert visitors into customers, not merely to build awareness.

10

STAND OUT FROM YOUR COMPETITION WITH THE POWER OF VIDEO

"No matter what you do,
your job is to tell your story."

- Gary Vaynerchuk

Throughout all of your marketing, you can leverage the power of video to connect with potential customers in a way that you simply can't through other mediums. There's something about the combination of audio and video combined that reaches people on an emotional level in a way that other media can't.

In this chapter, you'll learn where you can implement video in your digital marketing to stand out from the competition, how to get started, and when to hire a professional or do it yourself.

For Purchases Requiring a High Level of Trust and Investment, Video Can Make All the Difference

If your product or service is expensive, new, controversial, complicated, or otherwise misunderstood, video can help educate potential buyers about the benefits you have to offer. Chiropractic is one industry that falls into that category, for example.

For many people, chiropractic is scary, potentially dangerous, and questionably effective. There are many bad chiropractors out there, just like there are many bad marketers, mechanics, or any service provider. There are lots of horror stories of people who have a back injury that is made WORSE by a chiropractor.

I did marketing work with Dr. Simon Dove, a chiropractor in Fort Collins, Colorado, whose practice was having success growing primarily through referrals. The challenge he was facing was that leads that came from other marketing sources, and even sometimes referrals, didn't understand how his alternative approach to chiropractic could really help them with their ailments.

Dr. Dove offers a type of chiropractic called Network Spinal Analysis (NSA). Unlike other forms of chiropractic, in which the patient is adjusted in a way that makes a "crack," NSA is more so a series of light touches along the spine.

When people hear or see this, they assume that the doctor isn't actually doing anything, which presents a major sales and marketing challenge!

Although Dr. Dove was doing transformational work that improved the lives of his patients, he wasn't getting enough new patients to meet his income goals. And while he had a lot of website traffic and strong Google rankings, he was in a market saturated with competition. There are 20 pages of Google Maps results for "Fort Collins chiropractor," dozens who practice literally within miles of his location. He needed to do something to stand out and *convert the traffic on his site into leads and customers.*

People Remember Stories, Not Statistics

Leverage Video Testimonials to Make the Sale

We could have produced a video interviewing Dr. Dove geeking out about the technicalities of network spinal analysis, how smart he is, how educated he is, the statistics about chiropractic, and the details of the spine and how subluxations happen. But no one cares about that. *They just want to feel better* and they want to *trust that the solution they choose will make them feel better.*

While you're saying that your products and services are great, it's a whole different story when someone else says they are. Video testimonials, especially from a recognized authority or even from someone who is just like your ideal client, can help solidify a sale.

Interview People Who Fit Your Ideal Target Markets

Think about — who are my most profitable customers? How old are they? Are they male or female? Who actually makes the purchase, and what's most important to them?

We placed Dr. Dove's ideal customers into three categories: seniors, pregnant mothers or women who recently had children, and athletes with injuries. In his branding video — one installment in a series Ramblin Jackson produced — we interviewed one of each of those people about their experience.

The impact of sharing those stories in the form of professional video on Dr. Dove's business was astonishing. Here's what he had to say two years after implementing the videos:

> "*I definitely think the videos that I've shot have impacted my business in a fantastic way and impacted my bottom line. I would say, easily, every month I have several people come in and tell me, 'The reason I came in here was because of the information that I got on the video.' And I was actually a little shocked.*

"I knew it was going to be good and I knew I wanted it to stay modern. That was one of my big things. I wanted to set myself as a thriving business that keeps up with the times. And you know when you go to a web site of a very well-known prominent business, they always have some video clips at your access, so that was my big pursuit.

"I'm quite pleased that I see people come in every month people and say, 'That video made a difference. That's why I actually chose you as my chiropractor over the other chiropractors in town.'

"I've been doing this for 16 years. In the two years since making the video, I've noticed a little sense of ease, almost like we've gotten some work done before they even come in to the place. Because once I start talking to them, they have actually said some things that I've said on the video. Or they start talking to me as if they already know me. So it makes it really easy, and fun."

See the full video interview with Dr. Simon Dove about how video helped him increase his sales at ramblinjackson.com/results/

How to Recruit Top
Employees with Video

Recruiting, like selling anything else in your business, is a marketing activity. You want the *best* customers and clients, and you absolutely want the *best* employees. While video is a great way to market to new customers, it can also be an effective tool for marketing to new employees.

Great employees will do their research on places they want to work and then apply to them. Not only do you have competition in acquiring customers who are considering other companies that offer products and services similar to yours, you also have competition with those companies from a hiring standpoint.

What's it like to work at your company?

Forget what the CEO says — let's hear from the employees.

Just as letting your customers explain why they chose your products or services over a competitor's is better than hearing from the owner of the company, it's also way better when your employees endorse working at your company.

A recruiting video featuring interviews with your favorite employees can help attract similar candidates, and it can also help weed out people who may not be attracted to your work culture.

Case in point, check out Ramblin Jackson's "Why You Should Work At Ramblin Jackson" on YouTube or at ramblinjackson.com/jobs/.

Where You Should Host Your Videos + How to Embed Them on Your Website

Today, there are literally hundreds of places you can host your video, and at not much expense — from social media sites such as Facebook, Instagram, and Twitter, to dedicated video hosting sites like YouTube, Wistia, and Vimeo. So, which should you use? Most of them have their strong points, so it all comes down to what you want to achieve with your video.

Here are my top picks:

Wistia. This is the site Ramblin Jackson likes to use for the majority of our videos. In fact, if you watch a video on our website, you'll likely see it play from Wistia. This service has several different pricing options and is ideal for videos where people are a little further down the purchase funnel and visiting deeper pages on your website.

Among the benefits of Wistia's professional video hosting, it offers:

- **HubSpot integration**, which lets you see who is viewing your videos. It even allows for automated follow-up to site visitors at certain engagement levels.

- **Advanced customization**, which enables you to choose custom thumbnails, call to action links, and even email lead capture using its Turnstile feature.

If you're looking to learn more about video production as a whole, Wistia also features some helpful training videos and regularly shares educational tips.

While not perfect — and what internet service is? — Wistia has proven to be a solid choice for our use.

YouTube. Likely, the most well-known video host worldwide, YouTube continues to grow in popularity as more and more people cut the cord and turn to the internet for their entertainment.

But, more than that, YouTube — owned by Google — is also the number two search engine in the world, with people searching it for information about every subject imaginable. (And some you're probably better off not imagining for that matter.) That means it can be an optimal place to upload videos to benefit your SEO.

Among the other benefits:

YouTube is great for branding videos, Q&A videos like the Ask Swenk Show, and vloggers. (My personal favorite is Casey Neistat, an up-and-coming YouTube star who recently surpassed five million subscribers!)

Facebook. While its video view metrics have recently been called into question, this social media platform can still prove incredibly effective for video. Indeed, Mark Zuckerberg told BuzzFeed news this past April that he "…wouldn't be surprised if you fast-forward five years and most of the content that people see on Facebook and are sharing on a day-to-day basis is video." Among the benefits:

- Videos uploaded directly to Facebook get more views than links to YouTube videos shared on Facebook.

- You can do advanced Facebook Advertising targeted to your ideal audience for a very small investment and reach thousands of people!

How to Decide Where to Host Your Videos

If you're embedding videos on your website, we recommend hosting with a professional service like Wistia. This will ensure high-quality playback for your audience and give you advanced analytics.

For branding videos and video blogs, grow your subscription base with YouTube and start your own business channel.

Finally, **absolutely leverage Facebook for video!** Facebook video ads, in particular, are extremely effective and, when coupled with Facebook's Lead Generation campaigns, enable you to ramp up leads for your business quickly.

In my opinion, *where* you host your video should be driven by *what it needs to achieve* for your business and where people are in the sales funnel.

5 DIY Smartphone Tips to Produce Quality Video on a Budget

For the last ten years or so, camera equipment and editing software have become more and more available and affordable. The latest iPhones and Androids are pretty spectacular and, with many basic photography principles and some inexpensive smartphone accessories, you can produce a reasonably decent video.

Here are some tips to help:

1. Hold Your Phone Horizontally

Vertical (portrait) video is the scourge of non-professional online video, and it's easily preventable. Just hold your phone horizontally, in landscape mode. Shooting your video with your phone horizontal will keep those weird bars from appearing on each side, which helps it play nicely on wide desktop screens.

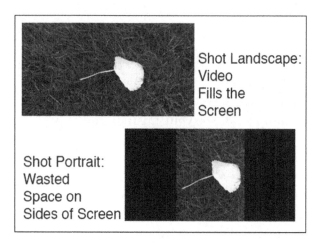

Here's a screenshot of a video a local garden center posted. You can only see part of their new goldfish in the pond. Wouldn't it be better to see the whole thing?

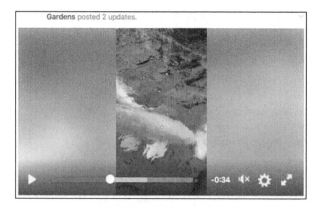

2. Use an External Mic + Lights

This can be as simple as using the earbuds that come with your smartphone and the microphone feature of those earbuds. Or, you can use a wireless lavalier microphone setup which can start on the low end around $40 and range all the way up to a Sennheiser wireless system like the one we use at Ramblin Jackson, which is currently in the $700 range (and worth every penny, IMO, having had it for 7+ years). A wireless microphone setup will cost you some money and add a little extra time to set up at each video shoot, but gives you the freedom to use your phone to record from longer distances. An in-between item is a more affordable wired lavalier mic (available on Amazon for $25 to $75).

For lights, this could be as simple as this LED light that screws into the iPhone tripod mount. While the model shown below is no longer available on Amazon, there are plenty just like it. A little bit of light goes a long way toward improving your video's quality.

3. Use a Tripod

While today's smartphones do a good job at smoothing out motion, they still won't completely offset the negative effects of a shaky hand. While there is a time and place for handheld or selfie stick videos — such as if you're on the road or at a tradeshow showing behind the scenes — in general, using a tripod makes a video look 10 times as legit as handheld video. (I'm a big fan of the Joby tripod mount and Manfrotto tripods.)

4. Pay Attention to Your Background

Pay attention to your surroundings, especially your background. This can be as simple as avoiding windows when you shoot so your subject doesn't appear in silhouette or the background isn't blown out behind you.

5. Choose a Subject That Adds Value or Answers a Question

Have something interesting to talk about. A lot of people make the mistake of recording videos about very little, subject-matter speaking. Videos like these are boring to watch, and most people just won't do it. Research your topic, spend time on scripting and planning, and record something that is actually worth watching.

Download the DIY video gear.
See the section on how to write blogs
in the Social Media chapter for ideas
on generating blog post or video ideas,
and check out my list of resources for
DIY Video gear + links to them on
Amazon at: ramblinjackson.com/videoguide/.

When to Hire a Professional Video Production Company

There's a lot more that goes into producing a great video than equipment, and there are certainly times when a DIY video is worse than no video at all. While DIY video can be great for quick social media clips, which I've outlined below, there are definitely videos for which you'll want to hire a professional.

A professional video producer *is a marketer who will help you craft content to achieve a specific business objective.* There is so much that goes into writing a powerful story, weeding out the junk, and editing a beautiful video that will take far more time and talent than you likely have as a small business owner.

Hire a Pro for Pieces You'll Use Every Day As Part of Your Sales

If you're going to use video on one of the top 20% of your web pages or nearly every day for a sales presentation, it's worth investing in a professional video. A professional video can establish your business as credible, trustworthy, and capable.

1. Branding Videos

A short video that communicates the value you offer to your clients, your core values, and what makes your business different is a great thing to have on your website homepage, YouTube channel, and Facebook page.

I recommend a 90- to 120-second video that quickly establishes confidence in your business. For Ramblin Jackson, we have a kind of weird western video with a man that looks like Sam Elliot from The Big Lebowski.

It tells our story in a fun way that still highlights what makes us better. I can tell from my Wistia/HubSpot analytics that *buyers* watch this video before contacting us, and so do most of our job candidates. Search "The Legend of Ramblin Jackson" or visit ramblinjackson.com to see this.

2. Customer Testimonials

You can certainly shoot customer testimonials on a smartphone — and you should if it's the only chance you'll get. If you implement some of the DIY best practices mentioned below, you can even get some good ones.

But for something that's going to be a staple in your marketing and in prominent pages on your website, having a well-lit, properly mic'd, and professionally-edited testimonial video can really be a cornerstone in your marketing. If you're in a service business or selling B2B, having professional customer testimonial videos could be your most impactful asset.

3. Product Videos

If your business sells a special product, you could use a professional video to help customers understand its features and benefits. Another advantage of making product videos is SEO. If people search for "XYZ Products in Boulder," that could be the title you use on YouTube, which then ranks in search engines, particularly Google.

4. Service Videos

Ideally, you'd have a professional video on each service page of your website. A short video can help people understand the benefits of your services, educate them on the process, and reaffirm that you are the best service provider among your peers. Including a short customer testimonial is an excellent way to pair education and a customer story to position yourself as an expert.

5. Non-profit Fundraising Videos

If you're a non-profit, it's a given that you have to raise money. Period. *All sales are based on emotion — including donations to non-profits.*

If your non-profit does work with people in need, there's a strong chance that you have some compelling, emotional stories that if told correctly, would motivate people to donate. WonderBound, a non-profit ballet school in Denver, has a program called Dance From The Heart that helps kids in poverty in the area get scholarships to dance classes. They credit a professional video we produced as being the difference maker in meeting their fundraising goals.

"Our event called Dance From The Heart is an annual fundraising event that benefits our community programs. I will say that one of the key elements to the success of the event is the video. When we had a video done by Ramblin Jackson, there was not a dry eye in the house.

"The other part about the video that so many people who do these fundraisers mentioned that the way it was timed, the way it all fit together, the slight musical changes, the smallest little details are what make that video really do the job it's supposed to, which is help fund these programs, which are essential to the arts in children's lives.

"We've had people do it in the past without as much success. For me, it's Ramblin Jackson all the way."

- Dawn Fay, WonderBound

The video is compelling because not only does it interview some of the directors about the background and purpose of the program but it also profiles the mothers of Riley and Abigail, two special needs girls who practice dance in

WonderBound's Ballet Expressions classes. The video interviews them about the impact.

"If this class didn't exist, there would be a huge void in our lives," Abigail's mother said.

"We've been looking for dance classes for three years before we found this. As a parent, not being able to fulfill that desire was tough on me. Having that class in our community and having that opportunity for her to participate is really priceless for us," Riley's mother said.

Their stories, coupled with beautiful cello music, tugs on the heartstrings... and opens checkbooks.

(See the video at ramblinjackson.com/results/)

Create Engaging Social Media Posts with Video

Smartphone video is perfect for behind the scenes, "spur of the moment, and short video clips to give your followers a sense of what your business is like. Posting short video clips on Facebook and Instagram from your smartphone can add engaging content, which you can repurpose as b-roll in future video edits or even embed on your website.

Facebook Live

Facebook Live is kind of like a live radio or TV broadcast on which people can comment. This can be a fun thing to do as a Q&A before an upcoming workshop, while you're mentioning changes in your industry, and more. Facebook Live is now available for desktop, but originally came out just on their mobile app.

One effective way of getting leads for your business with Facebook Live is to have a link in the status update to a lead generation or event registration page.

In the example below, I did a Facebook Live video for the Q&A session following a digital marketing trends workshop. The workshop participants asked their question to me in-person, in addition to questions from people commenting on Facebook.

This extended the Q&A everywhere, and people as far as Boston were viewing! Afterwards, we ran a Facebook ad retargeting the people who had visited our website and included a link in the update, which funneled people into our marketing automation platform.

Instagram Videos

At this time, you can create up to 60-second videos on Instagram. One of the things I like about Instagram videos is that they can give users a behind the scenes look at a local or national brand.

Instagram videos could consists of a short clip of an employee, an exercise (if you're a Pilates studio, for instance), recipes... or anything really. By using the right hashtags, you quickly get visibility in front of people who are interested in what you offer. You can also embed your Instagram videos into blog posts or pages on your website.

Use Video in Email Marketing to Boost Opens and Click-thru Rates

If you're sending out email marketing campaigns, incorporating video is a hot business. Using the word "video" in the subject line has been proven to improve open rates (the number of people who open your email that received it), and having a thumbnail of the video in the email has been shown to increase click-thru rates (the number of people who open the email that click on something, such as a link).

At Ramblin Jackson, we've been sending out a video every Friday for the past six years called Friday's Ramblin Roundup. It's short, fun, and helpful to our clients. We share industry trends, tips for social media, and elements that position us as experts in the eye of our clients.

Use video email campaigns to:

- Welcome new clients;

- Introduce your team;

- Run a lead generation campaign;

- Announce new products and services;

- Reactivate old clients.

When you send out a video email campaign don't try to embed the video in the email. Instead, take a screenshot of the video and have that image link to the blog post where you have it embedded.

I recommend embedding the video to a blog post or page on your website and link to that versus linking to YouTube. (Unless you want people to go to YouTube and start watching cat videos!)

Here's an example of a recent Friday's Ramblin Roundup email campaign. In this example, I included a selfie from MozCon Local 2017 with Google My Business UX Writer Willys DeVoll and GetFiveStars founder and Local SEO legend Mike Blumenthal.

I always use an image of me or one of my staff in the video thumbnail because a Wistia study and my own tests have shown that people click-thru to

these videos more than video thumbnails with just
text or other less-personal imagery.

What's new in local SEO?

A couple weeks ago I attended MozCon Local, a digital marketing conference
in Seattle all about local search. I'm sure you don't want to geek out on all 42

From your website, social media, email marketing,
online advertising, and offline marketing, video can
be a powerful tool in your marketing arsenal. Video
can add color to your lead generation, to your
employee recruiting, and even to operational needs
like employee onboarding, training, and more.

Key Takeaways From Stand Out From Your Competition With The Power of Video

- Video taps into emotion in a powerful way that other media simply can't.

- People remember stories over statistics. Let your best customers and employees tell the stories for you.

- Hire a professional for core video pieces like sales, branding, and fundraising videos.

- Go for it! Make some videos on your smartphone! Check out our DIY smartphone video guide at ramblinjackson.com/videoguide/.

- Hold your phone horizontally in landscape mode, use a tripod, lighting, and a lapel mic for better quality DIY videos.

- Plan the goal of the video before you produce it.

- Leverage the power of video in your website, social media, and email marketing.

11

MEASURE RESULTS

"If you can't measure it,
you can't improve it."

- Peter Drucker

If you're investing in marketing, it should produce measurable results for your business. How else would you know what's working and what isn't, what should be kept and what should be cut? In this chapter, you'll learn a few ideas for how to measure the results of your digital marketing to make better business decisions.

Local Business Digital Marketing Key Performance Indicators (KPIs)

To know if your marketing is actually working, you need to measure outcomes. As marketing strategist and author Dan Kennedy says in his "10

Commandments of Direct Response Marketing"–
"Results Rule."

What you measure and how you grade your
marketing will be very different depending on what
you sell, your sales process, buying cycle, etc.
Measuring the marketing for a garden center
would differ from that of a landscaper, and a pizza
shop wouldn't be the same as a retail store or
dentist. In any case, it's important that you set and
communicate with your marketing team the key
performance indicators (KPIs) *at the start* of
creating your digital marketing plans.

Examples of Local Business KPIs:

- # of driving directions from Google My
  Business or Yelp Analytics;

- # of inbound telephone calls measured with
  your phone reports or a call tracking
  software like CallRail;

- # of repeat customers measured in your
  point of sale, CRM, or bookkeeping program;

- # of new patients;

- Position (ranking) on Google for top
  keywords measured using keyword ranking
  software like Moz Analytics or Google
  Search Console;

- # of leads measured in your sales CRM such
  as HubSpot or Infusionsoft;

- # of downloads or opt-ins measured from your Google Analytics Event Goals or email marketing software;

- # of store visits or walk-ins measured manually (if you're a maniac) or through a software like Aislelabs or Shoppertrak;

- Percentage of traffic to your website from organic search measured in Google Analytics.

While things like Facebook post engagement can be helpful at improving your posts, the KPIs listed above are the types of metrics that are a little closer at indicating what's actually happening in the business.

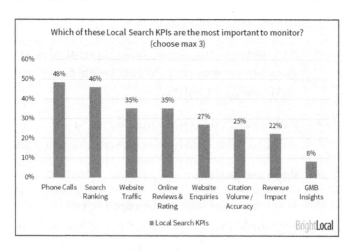

According to a survey of BrightLocal users,[1] phone calls and search rankings were rated as the top two most important KPIs for measuring local search marketing. (Note that this survey was taken by

BrightLocal users who consisted of marketers and business owners and that it is specific to local SEO, not all digital marketing.)

I was surprised to see that revenue impact wasn't ranked higher, however. I agree that, in general, phone calls and search ranking should be the top KPIs *when evaluating local search marketing initiatives.*

There is much that happens after the phone call that is outside of the local SEO marketer's control, such as: did the company answer the telephone (60% don't!), was the call handled well (most businesses have little sales training), did the receptionist ask the potential patient to book an appointment (or just answer their question about whether or not your dental office offers veneers), and so on? What do you think?

For some businesses, such as retail shops, *driving directions* may be a higher prioritized KPI. For a restaurant, *online reservations* may be the higher priority.

You should think about your entire customer journey and life cycle to determine the KPIs that are most meaningful to your business. If possible, track it all the way through to the sale to get the best understanding of how your marketing dollars are working for you. In any case, you can't expect to get more leads/appointments/phone calls/reservations/etc. from people finding you on

Google if you're not ranking in a highly visible position.

The Growing Challenge with Tracking Local SEO Rankings

While search ranking is a useful metric, it is becoming more complex to track with 100% accuracy for local businesses because <u>proximity to the device is now the #1 ranking factor for map results</u>, according to the 2017 Moz Local Search Ranking Factors Survey.[2]

That means how close a business is to the device making the search, is the top ranking factor — so a person in south Chicago would see entirely different search results for "best pizza" than a person searching in north Chicago.

While there ARE tools out there that can track all of those things, they're super expensive and not entirely reliable. Besides, there's nothing you can control about where a person is searching from. What you can control are the things that will help that person find you, such as Name, Address, and Phone (NAP) consistency, content on your website, links, etc.; so focus your time on that.

Is tracking keyword rankings still meaningful if we can't 100% track the map results due to varying proximities? Yes, absolutely. Tracking keyword rankings can still give us actionable insight as to the *trends* of our keyword positioning over time, which we can use to focus our SEO efforts and PPC initiatives.

"How Did You Hear of Us?"

If you're not asking your customers how they heard of you, it's time to start!

This question must be part of your sales script that you train your salespeople to use, and you must have a method for easily collecting and recording this information.

This method could be as simple as a piece of paper near the telephone at your front desk with tick marks next to the number of calls from each marketing source, or as advanced as call recording and call tracking software integrated with your CRM. Whatever you do, develop a system that your employees will actually use, and make time to interpret the data.

Asking "How did you hear of us?" can produce a goldmine of information.

Oh, I found you on Google...

Great! Do you remember what you were searching for?

Knowing what people were searching for can help you know if your SEO is working. Plus, it can help you focus some additional blog posts and SEO content around that keyword phrase. OR, if you're getting the WRONG leads — such as if you're a high-end custom jewelry store and people are finding you for "watch repair" when you don't even offer that service — you can take a look at your SEO and remove whatever content may be helping you rank for that.

If the new customer is a referral, ask who referred them — and then send that person a gift, thank you card, or at least call them to say thanks. I've found that rewarding people who send referrals, or at least telling them thank you, has helped them send even more referrals along the way.

Many people don't remember.

Not all of your customers or clients are small business owners or marketers. Most people have no idea how SEO works and wouldn't even think to remember what they searched to find you. They may just think they found you on "the internet," when they actually searched on Yelp. Take whatever your customers tell you about how they found you with a grain of salt.

Measuring Marketing's Impact on Revenue

If you're in an e-commerce business making sales through an online shopping cart, you can track nearly every dollar back to the source. You could also track "assisted conversions" — web pages, videos, advertisements, or remarketing ads that people see after their first visit to your site — that may have contributed to the sale.

It's much more black and white as to what's working and what isn't. For digital marketing for local businesses such as retail or service area businesses — with the exception of direct response advertising campaigns in which people are redeeming a specific offer promoted in limited channels — it's much harder to track every marketing dollar to a sale.

Marketing dollars are much more trackable from service businesses with fewer, larger transactions. A landscaper who has +/- 100 orders in a year should be able track his marketing much more easily than, say, a garden center that may see hundreds of customers a DAY during its spring rush.

Here are a few ways you can track your marketing to sales:

Use a Sales CRM like HubSpot

HubSpot has a (mostly) free Sales CRM. CRM stands for Customer Relationship Management system -- it's essentially a program where you can log your customer contact information as well as notes, emails, and call records. You can connect it to the contact forms on your website, add customer details, and have fields for marketing sources. With their Sales Pro version (which I personally love), you can log and record calls, use email templates, and more. And with their Marketing Product, you can track people's behavior on your website, including what pages people have viewed. (There's even a Wistia integration to show you what videos people have viewed.)

Using a sales CRM is critical, in my opinion, for any organization that does B2B sales or has a multi-stage sales process, such as a landscaper, HVAC contractor, or home service business.

At Ramblin Jackson, we have a custom field for the marketing source. It's required for our account managers to fill out this field in order for them to get paid for a sale. The data is then inputted into QuickBooks. In a matter of minutes, I could tell you the original marketing source of every single customer we have.

Put Custom Fields in Your Point of Sale

If you have a point of sale (POS), there's likely a field for marketing or an opportunity to add a custom field. Teach your front desk people how to fill this in as this can help you measure long-term ROI from marketing.

How much do your customers spend over time? How many visits do they have? Which marketing brings in customers who spend the most or visit the most? Which marketing brings in the lowest paying customers?

Run Coupon/Offer Redemption Campaigns

Running any kind of coupon or discount "if you mention this ad" campaign can be an easy way of tracking marketing campaigns.

How to Track Marketing Sources in QuickBooks Online (for Service Businesses)

Note: This information is specific to *QuickBooks Online*, which is different from QuickBooks desktop software. Many of the principles listed below will still apply

1. Make a list of all your marketing

First, write down the possible marketing categories. You can get as specific or as broad as you'd like. Remember, it's only meaningful if you're able to interpret the data and take action on it.

For example you could track:

- **Search** - customers who find you on search engines;

- **Sponsorship** - customers who found you from an in-kind sponsorship;

- **Trade show** - customers who found you as a result of the various trade shows;

- **Public speaking** - customers who found you as a result of a public speaking engagement;

- **Print advertising** - customers who found you as a result of your print ads;

- **Referral** - customers who found you as a result of word-of-mouth;

- **Outbound** - cold calling, prospecting for new business.

Additionally, you could track with another field with Custom Form Styles for things like New Customer vs. Repeat Customer; Salesperson; and more.

2. Create a Territory Field with dropdown options using the Location Tracking

- Click the Gear Icon in the upper right corner >>> click All Lists

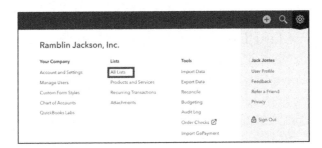

- All Lists >>> Territories

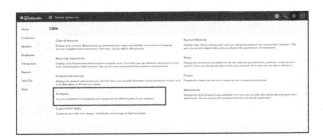

- Add new territories for each of the Marketing Sources from your list

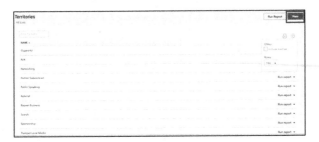

3. Require that ALL invoices be created with this information, and select the Territory on each invoice

Now that you have your tracking system setup, you need to feed it data.

Make it a company policy that this information is updated each and every time an invoice is created. Otherwise, it just won't happen. If you have salespeople who are selling to clients and creating or requesting invoice creation, make them provide this marketing data if they want to get paid.

At Ramblin Jackson, when our account managers request an invoice, we have a cool template setup using HubSpot Sales PRO's email templates. It automatically pulls the Marketing Source (and relevant customer contact info) from the client's HubSpot Contact Record into an email that is sent to our bookkeeper who then creates an invoice and inputs the data. By having it templated, and also required, we have accurate invoicing every single time without a lot of manual data entry or need to think or remember.

4. Run a report by territory

Reports >>> Sales by Class Summary

Customize the "Display Columns By" dropdown item to "Territories," and then set the date range, select cash or accrual, and run the report.

From there, you can geek out on your data, export it to Excel, make pretty graphs, and evaluate which marketing is bringing in the best customers.

5. Advanced: Track your expenses with marketing and a subcategory for the Marketing Sources above.

After reading *80/20 Sales And Marketing* by Perry Marshall (which is an incredible book you should read right after you finish this one), I decided to do a deep dive on my own analytics — specifically, and discovered that nearly 80% of the revenue I generated from public speaking came from just one conference nearly five years ago. After discovering that, I shifted the focus of my agency to focus my outbound marketing in a particular niche vertical.

I spoke at the conference twice and then had a booth there the following two years. I'm now able to use this information when budgeting for a tradeshow. (Takeaway: speaking at an association conference or tradeshow can have HUGE results vs. speaking at a general "business" conference.)

You can also use this data to track metrics like customer retention. Which marketing produces the BEST long-lasting, highest paying customers?

Of course, you'll need to customize your QuickBooks and invoicing to your own business needs and processes. I recommend chatting with your bookkeeper about this or contacting QuickBooks customer support (or the support team at whatever bookkeeping software you use).

> Do this early in your business
> so you start collecting good data!

How to Measure against Expenses and Consider the PROFIT Generated from Lifetime Value (LTV) per Customer

---

The Website is like a ¾ ton Pickup Truck
It's a Rugged Piece of Equipment
You'll Use for YEARS

Dear Business Owner,
It's time to get a new truck.
Let's build a good one that's done right
the first time and lasts a long time!

How many new customers would it take to pay back a $30,000 investment in a marketing program?

Average Lifetime Value Per Customer (LTV)	$10,000
Net Profit Margin	30%
Net Profit Of One (1) Customer	$3,000

You would need 10 new customers to make back your $30,000 investment in a marketing program.

Would you expect to do more than 10 new customers total over the next five years from this?

Would it be worth investing a few thousand more in our proven process to have a lasting, quality SEO and Marketing Program that you can build on?

Once you start factoring in your lifetime value, and *profit margin* -- not just gross revenue generated, it can help you look at your marketing initiatives more clearly. If the required investment for a marketing asset -- like a fully optimized website that generated qualified leads every day to your business -- and you used that website for at least five years, the above illustration can help you determine if it's a wise investment.

The Data Won't Be Perfect

There will likely be large margin of error and this data will be imperfect. Often, your customers won't remember specifically how they found you when you ask, "How did you hear of us?" (They might even lie or make up an answer!)

Did they see your ad on a bus or find you online? Did a friend refer them? Perhaps they saw some social media posts or an ad for your direct response offer but forget to redeem it and came in to your store anyhow?

Whatever their answer, you can still get a sense of what's working and what's not by at least tracking your marketing at a broad level like I've shown you. The metrics will vary for every business.

Key Takeaways From Measuring Results

- Develop an easy-to-implement means of collecting "how did you hear of us?"

- Put "how did you hear of us" data into QuickBooks or your accounting program with each invoice creation.

- Require your sales and customer service staff to help track this.

- Measure results based on Lifetime Value and be sure to factor in your Profit margin

- Set specific goals at the start of working with marketing vendors as well as timeline for results

- Tweak what isn't working or cut it!

12

MAKE THE SALE

"Timid salesmen have skinny kids."

- Zig Ziglar

Up to now, this book has primarily been about marketing tactics to get people to call you, contact you, or discover your business. While being FOUND is important, it doesn't matter unless you sell something! This chapter will show you how to do that, in two ways: by answering the telephone and setting up an easy to follow sales process.

Dude, Answer Your Telephone

With all this hassle to get people to find or contact you, I'm amazed by how many businesses don't actually answer the telephone. If you're not going to answer the phone, why bother doing all of this marketing or even be in business at all?

While online scheduling, online chat, email, and SMS are growing trends of communication that you need to respond to quickly, the most serious buyers and potential customers will contact you on the telephone.

This is especially true for medical practices, dental offices, or service area businesses in which a prospective customer may have additional questions to ask before they make their final decision to do business with you.

Ask any business owner:
Phone leads rule.

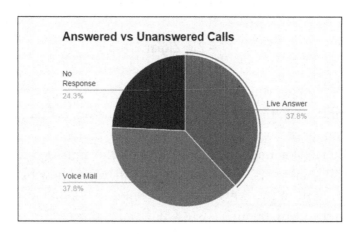

According to a recent study by 411 Locals,[1] 62% of calls to small businesses go entirely unanswered. No answer! What a wasted opportunity!

As a small business owner, I know how busy things can get. You can feel overwhelmed at times. Maybe you are in a meeting with a client or otherwise unavailable to answer your phone, and all of your staff is tied up as well. But as busy as you get, that's no excuse for not answering the phone.

Pro Tip: If someone in your shop can't answer the phone after a certain number of rings, consider routing the call to a virtual receptionist or answering service.

There are pay-as-you-go programs that are quite affordable. This way, your calls get answered and someone trained to answer basic questions can help you get a new customer or at least collect their info so you can call them back.

Save $75 With CallRuby
Have your phone answered professionally even when you're not there.
Increase sales. Save time.
Focus on your work.

Save $75 off your first month when you use promo code RAMBLIN at
callruby.com/ramblin/

Respond to Leads within One Hour to Increase Sales Conversion 7x

Whatever you do, act fast. Responding to an inbound sales lead from a prospective customer within an hour increases your likelihood of making the sale by 7x, according to a study published in the Harvard Business Review[2].

A study by the Harvard Business Journal shows that if you respond to a lead within one hour – you increase your sales conversion 7x. This doesn't mean you need to respond right away and have a full sales conversation — maybe you respond and schedule an appointment for that.

Leverage Templates, Scripts, and Automation Whenever Possible to Save Time

Responding within an hour and all sounds great — and likely, you can templatize the way you do it to save time. Set up an Auto-reply from your website contact form. If possible, leverage your CRM to personalize the subject line and response. Get text message notifications when your website contact form is completed. You can also use canned messages or a sales CRM to have ready-to-go templates that save you a ton of time!

Develop and Manage a Sales Process

So you've trained your staff to answer the telephone. Now what? What should they say? A surprising number of businesses I work with don't have any sales training or sales process to follow.

While there are a lot of different methodologies behind sales, the methodology I prefer to use is called "Baseline Selling," Created by author Dave Kurlan.[3] "Baseline Selling" is essentially a sales framework using the concepts of baseball.

- 1st Base = Have an appointment.

- 2nd Base = They have what you need, there is urgency, and you have shown speed on the bases (what Kurlan refers to as the S.O.B. Quality[4]).

- 3rd Base = The prospect is completely qualified to do business with you and you are completely qualified to do business with the prospect.

- Home = You have presented a perfect solution, appropriate for their budget, and they have made a decision to buy from you.

I originally discovered Baseline Selling from my sales management coach, Wayne Herring, from

Stronger Sales People. What I like about Baseline Selling is that you can adapt it to just about any existing sales process.

The best part is that it can simplify the sales process in a way that a good salesperson can learn and remember easily. (It's no secret that many sales processes are so complicated that people don't remember how to use them.)

I highly recommend that you check out Kurlan's book, *Baseline Selling: How to Become a Sales Superstar by Using What You Already Know About the Game of Baseball.*

While Baseline Selling may be more relevant to a service area business, like a landscaper than a retailer, what matters most is that your entire company — especially the people doing your marketing and, absolutely, the folks answering the telephone — understand how your sales process works and how they fit into it.

Show up on Time

The best way to earn someone's trust is to show up on time at the beginning of the relationship and to be respectful of their most precious asset: their time. Contractors are notorious for showing up late

— within huge time windows — and sending proposals late. Showing up on time will make you ten times easier to work with and help you earn the sale.

At Ramblin Jackson, one of our core values is On-Time And Prepared To Add Value. Unlike most flakey marketers in our industry, we promise to be on-time for all meetings. To make it fun, we have a Beef Jerky Club. Yep, if we're ever late for a meeting – we will send you high quality beef jerky in the mail. **See if you qualify for our Jerky Club at ramblinjackson.com/jerky/**

Key Takeaways From Make The Sale

- Digital Marketing is pointless unless your business is capable of making the sale.

- Answer the telephone!

- Respond to inbound leads within an hour to increase your sales by 7x.

- Develop a written sales process.

- Train your salespeople, receptionists, and marketing team on your sales process.

13

BEYOND DIGITAL MARKETING: BE EXCELLENT. BE LOCAL.

"We make a living by what we get,
but we make a life by what we give."

- Winston Churchill

Digital marketing, for all its value, is only one part of what makes local businesses successful. It's what they do *offline* — how they treat their customers, employees, and community — that really matters.

The most successful businesses I work with see themselves as *brands*. They place great emphasis on providing excellent customer service and are actively involved in their community. They strive to be the best at everything they do. THAT, combined with good digital marketing, is what makes them a success.

How to Deliver Exceptional Customer Service Experiences

One of my clients is The Sink, Boulder's oldest restaurant and bar. They're located on The Hill, a popular street near the University of Colorado Boulder campus in a one-hundred year old building whose walls are covered with the iconic artwork of Llloyd Kavich (with three Ls for the "L" of it!).

A lot of college students and local folks know The Sink has the best burgers and pizza in town, and they've been featured on high profile shows like Diners, Drive-ins, and Dives.

Once, a girl in the crowd spilled yogurt on President Barack Obama when he visited the restaurant. They soon released the POTUS burger in honor of the former president.

Despite having such high profile, rich history, and online mentions from powerful news websites, The Sink wasn't ranking on Google for "best pizza" and "best burger" searches, and owner Mark Heinritz was frustrated.

We analyzed their online reviews and found that they had a 3.5 or below average on a lot of the sites, such as TripAdvisor, Yelp, Facebook, and Google My Business (which pulls in review data from other sites).

If you eat at The Sink, you know that their burgers and pizza are top notch. What skews their reviews is that a lot of their late night clientele may have had too much to drink, became belligerent, and then wrote reviews. But drunken ramblings aside, there was some legitimate feedback in there about the customer service from the waitstaff.

Six months after my conversation with Mark, we had lunch together at The Sink, and took another look at his reviews. Here are the results:

- Yelp increased to 3.5 star average;

- TripAdvisor increased to 4 star average;

- Facebook increased to 4.4 star average;

- Google My Business increased to 4 star average (displaying as 3.9 because that number represents an aggregate of other review sites).

Increasing from 3.5 to 3.9 on Google may seem easy, but when you have 1,643 reviews across four major review sites (plus all the other smaller ones), it takes quite a bit to move the needle.

I asked Mark how he did it. He said that after really reading through and looking at the reviews, he knew that he needed to make a change, and he did. He rounded up all of his 50+ employees and pointed out the reviews. He made improving the experience of The Sink a priority and coached his waitstaff on how to handle complaints. In the coming months, customers noticed the improved experience which was reflected in The Sink's improving online review averages.

I was so proud of Mark and the Sink for *listening* to their reviews, taking action, and improving the quality of their customer service. THAT is the kind of power you have as a small business. THAT is the kind of change you can make.

A Harvard Business School survey[1] showed that a 1-star review difference on Yelp can equate to 5-9% impact on a restaurant's revenue.

You can bet that Mark's hustle to increase his review average will impact his bottom line from out-of-state tourists visiting Boulder looking for the "best burger near me." So many businesses ask, "What can I do to have better SEO?" but Mark knew the right question was, "How can I improve the *experience of coming to restaurant* to *earn* better reviews?"

What kind of experience do you offer your customers? Why should you rank for "best" searches, and why should you be in business for 100 years?

Be Part of the Community

Another way to succeed is to become actively involved in the community. Giving back to the community can take many forms, from volunteering to donating to or sponsoring an event to speaking at workshops and public gatherings.

While I don't think that the purpose of giving back is to get something in return, as a local small business, I absolutely think it's appropriate for you to consider how to make people aware of what you are doing in the community. It will help build even more awareness toward the cause you're supporting, perpetuate further donations, recruit more volunteers — and employees who share your values — and get your business some brand awareness (and, potentially, links) as a byproduct.

If your employees volunteer at an event, take photos and post them on social media. Bonus points if you can get photos with cute animals.

Make a short video while you're there–it's a great way to show people what your company values are, and build awareness for the nonprofit you support. Write a blog post on your website that links back to the nonprofit, and ask them to share the post from their social media, email newsletter, or website.

Local SEO Link Building Tip #1: Asking for a link back from the nonprofit or event sponsor's site is something many people overlook. However, getting such links is a huge part of ranking in search engines, so keep this in mind in your future community event sponsorships.

Often, when you sponsor an event, you can negotiate for what type of publicity you want, which can include an advertisement in the event flyer and other promotional materials. If you do get an advertisement, include a direct response offer.

Here's an example of an advertisement that we ran when we sponsored the "Women Who Light the Community" event, an annual award ceremony put on by the Boulder Chamber honoring women leaders in the community. (We've been the video production sponsor for the past seven years.)

The ad lists a landing page where people can opt-in to receive special content via email. This helps us get new leads and know if they came from the sponsorship.

Implementing basic direct response principles, such as a time-limited offer, gift with purchase if you bring in the ad, or a coupon to drive people into your store, will help you get a much better response from your sponsorship versus just slapping your logo on the flyer.

Host Your Own Events
and Speak At Others

Another way to actively participate in your community is to host and speak at events. When people see you speak, they view you as an authority on your topic.

One of the other benefits of incorporating events in your marketing is that even if people don't show up to the event, they will likely still hear about it and see it on social media.

If you speak at a high-profile event, always get cool photos to post on your social media, website, and email newsletter. Whenever possible, take pictures of people who have a high social profile and tag them online in the photo.

Take photos of the audience and post them as well. Just make sure they are OK with this so you don't upset people who don't want to be featured. Most will be supportive however, and may even share the photo from your page, which will generate even more visibility — for free!

Local SEO Link Building Tip #2: Leverage events to build backlinks to your website.

There are tons of online calendars from local newspapers that will list your event for free. Do a search for "events in *insert city name*" or "business events calendar + *city name*."

If you really want to rank well, host the event at your office. By doing this, you can find event calendars and citations that will list your name, address, and phone number, in addition to a link to your website.

> What do you do when there are 80 competitors in your business category in your city?
> Be the absolute best and make your customers feel special.

Because dental practices can become very profitable, many people open them. For example, there are more than 80 dentists listed on Google Maps for "Boulder dentists" — 80! And only three of those map results appear on front page Google search returns. The rest you have to click through to find.

If you're a dentist in Boulder, how do you compete?

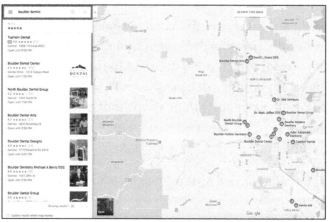

Sure, SEO is extremely effective for acquiring new dental patients.

People move and need a new dentist, and they search on Google to find one. People get new dental insurance and want a new dentist, and they, too, search on Google. People have a bad experience and need a new dentist — and they search on Google. People have kids who fall down and hit their teeth on the patio (like mine) and need a pediatric dentist. What do they do? Search on Google (and read every single review). Those are just a few of the many reasons people search Google for dentists.

That said, you can add "Boulder dentist" all you want all over your website. You can get all the links in the world. You can get all the reviews possible. You can mark up your site with schema. You can SEO the wazoo out of everything that can possibly be wazooed!

> But if you really deserve to rank number one and want to <u>earn the patient</u> over the other 79 competitors, you need to make people feel special and be the absolute best at what you do!

I recently had breakfast with Dr. Bob Murphy from North Boulder Dental Group. They've been a Ramblin Jackson client for a couple of years and we've been fortunate to collaborate with them on their SEO, website, and digital marketing.

Dr. Bob is an incredibly accomplished person who has been successful in business for over 30 years. I asked him what one thing contributed to his success the most over the years, and his answer was quite simple:

> *"We're in the relationship business with dentistry on the side."*

At North Boulder Dental Group, during your first visit, your doctor spends close to an hour meeting with you discussing your health goals and educating you about their practice philosophy. Who else does that?!

Even better, when you leave, they give you a rose. What do you do with a rose? Why, give it to your spouse, partner, or friend, put it in a vase and enjoy it for the rest of the week — and you certainly tell people about it. You remember *the way it made you feel when the dentist took the time to build rapport with you and how special you felt when you received the rose.*

People don't forget these types of experiences, and you earn Google reviews from them without even asking.

And that, my friends, is how you build a thriving business.

P.S. If you happen to be the best dentist in your market and want more people to find you online, check out ramblinjackson.com/dental or call us at (303) 544-2125.

Key Takeaways From Beyond Digital Marketing: Be Excellent. Be Local.

- Be the best at what you do.

- Coach your staff on how to deliver exceptional customer service.

- Participate in your community through sponsorships and events, and leverage those experiences for SEO and social media opportunities.

- Be a relationship business. Make the customer feel special.

14

GET STARTED WITH DIGITAL MARKETING

"The bitterness of poor quality
remains long after the sweetness
of low price is forgotten."

- Benjamin Franklin

As you can see from this book, there's quite a lot a
local business needs to do to successfully grow their
business with digital marketing. As a fellow small
business owner, I know what it's like to have rent,
staff to manage, bills to pay, and limited time.

It's important that you focus both your time and
your money on activities and investments that will
grow the business right away and for the long
term. You can't do it all in a day, or even a year. It
can take years to build up your marketing and
branding, and you'll never be quite "done." You've

got to get started somewhere, and this chapter will help you get moving in the right direction and prioritize which pieces to focus on in which order.

Focus:
Start by Building Your Foundation

Depending on where you're at in your business, some chapters in this book may be more relevant to you than others. Pick one that feels like it can make this biggest impact, read it and read it again. Choose and implement an action step and see how it goes.

To be truly successful, you'll need to build on a strong foundation. Take a look at this pyramid. Is your branding solid? Is your website well designed? Is your SEO dialed in? If you don't have those three elements in place, your foundation is weak. You *could* jump ahead to online advertising, but you may get diminished returns, and when your ad budget runs out -- so will your lead generation.

How do you build a strong foundation? You could do it yourself, hire freelancers, or work with an agency. Let's explore the pros and cons of each.

Take the Do-It-Yourself (DIY) Approach

If your business is small, scrappy, and just starting out, it could make sense for you to do the marketing yourself. Maybe you have a background in marketing and can come up with a strategy. Perhaps you also have the time, talent, and resources to do your own content, design, and implementation. If you do, rock on!

Things to consider before you DIY:

- Is this the highest and best use of your time as the leader of your company?

- Are there tasks that only you can do for your business, which aren't being completed because you're working on this?

- Do you keep putting this off even though you know it's important?

- Is the quality of your digital marketing as professional as it could be?

- Are you doing your SEO incorrectly and causing more harm than good?

- Most importantly: *are you capable of doing marketing that will generate the results you need to accomplish for your business?*

If your answers to these questions make you unsure of whether or not you should be doing the marketing yourself, chances are you probably shouldn't. So, let's explore the next option.

Have an Employee Do Your Digital Marketing

If you don't want to do the digital marketing, it may be possible for one of your employees to do so. If you go this route, make sure that he or she *has the time budgeted to do it regularly*. If digital marketing doesn't become part of their job description, then it will fall by the wayside.

I think there is a lot of marketing that your employees can do that would be difficult to outsource, such as:

- Posting spontaneous photos and short smartphone video clips to social media;

- Responding to negative reviews;

- Replying to website contact form submissions.

Also, some of your employees may have better writing skills and be able to contribute articles for the company blog, email newsletters, and other media.

The biggest mistake I see local businesses make when they go this route is that they don't set clear expectations, roles, and responsibilities. They also don't measure results. However, the worst mistake I see them make is that they don't give their employees adequate time to do this work — and digital marketing takes time when done correctly.

Sure, your 26-year-old employee probably has better computer and social media skills than you and may be faster at getting the job done, but that doesn't mean she can do effective *marketing* AND manage the front desk during your peak season without compromising one or the other.

Hire a Bunch of Freelancers

If you've decided that you should be focusing your time and your employees' time elsewhere and that hiring professionals for your marketing is a good idea, congratulations. You're way ahead of many, often unsuccessful business owners who hobble along with insufficient, incomplete, homemade marketing — to their own demise.

If you're ready to hire professional marketers, consider these questions:

- Do you know who to work with?

- Do you know where to find the right people, how to interview them, and how much to pay them?

- Do you have the time and bandwidth to do quality control, oversee, manage, and keep on track on all the different vendors?

- Will the outcome of hiring a bunch of different folks help build a unified, professional, and consistent brand?

If you have the time to recruit, interview, hire, train, and manage a bunch of different vendors and oversee all of their work, this could be a viable option.

> More times than not, most of the digital marketing problems businesses have are a result of *hiring the wrong person for the wrong job*.

- Website design is NOT website development;

- Website development is NOT search engine optimization (SEO);

- Search engine optimization is NOT social media marketing;

- And so on.

While everything I talk about in this book is related, each area of digital marketing requires its own, specialized skill-set. Having managed a digital agency for over nine years, and having hired and fired many digital marketing "professionals," I can tell you that it's very rare to find someone who has ALL the skills needed to successfully run all aspects of a company's digital marketing.

Among the skills needed are:

Strategy. Identifying a business's goals, challenges, and opportunities — and creating a solid plan to reach those goals through digital marketing.

Account Management. Managing the relationship with a client throughout the project and after to ensure they are feeling good about things and to identify opportunities.

Project Management. Getting all the work done on time and within budget, meeting deadlines, managing quality control, and keeping all the various team members on track.

Copywriting. Writing great content that keeps the target customer, the buyer's journey, and call to action firmly in mind.

Design. Making the website and marketing collateral look nice.

Other areas where specialized skills are needed include:

- Web development

- Search engine optimization

- Analytics

- Security and maintenance

- Hosting

And the list goes on... and on... and on.

The people who can do all of those things are called Unicorns in the industry. And they are literally as rare as unicorns. I have met one and hired him to design my website. He went on to create a thriving Amazon store, information products, a bee business, and right now he's learning 3D programming.

Unicorns are extremely expensive — typically three to four times the cost of the high end of the range for any given talent — and they're also hard to retain.

Unicorns know their worth and will say no to most requests without charging an unreasonably high fee. They also tend to get bored easily and need to move on to learning a new skillset after they've mastered another. This makes them often unreliable and, typically, unsuited for either employment or being a vendor.

While it's unlikely you'll encounter a true Unicorn, it's highly probable you'll encounter someone who will lead you to believe that they are... Someone much more dangerous... a *Dude-in-a-Van!*

Beware of Dude-in-a-Van: The True Cost of Cheap Digital Marketing Vendors

Dude-in-a-Van might be your next door neighbor, brother-in-law's buddy, your friend from college who's into computers, your company's former IT guy, or even a graphic designer you met at a networking event.

To be clear, I was once a dude in a van. I had a minivan, in fact, to transport my band equipment. It was a red Pontiac minivan and its transmission blew out while I was on tour with my band in Salt Lake City. (No wonder Pontiac went out of business. Good riddance!)

It was on that fateful trip that I decided to strikeout on my own as a freelance copywriter and "social media strategist." After a couple years of freelancing, and with the help of some business coaches, lots of books and conferences, and years of 70+ hour weeks, I worked my way out of being a dude in a van into a digital agency owner with a team of specialists and a niche specialty: local SEO. Likely, you were a Dude-in-a-Van at one point. It's a rite of passage on your entrepreneurial journey to building an Enterprise.

Dude-in-a-Van exists in every industry. In landscaping, he is typically called "Chuck-In-A-Truck" — the guy with a couple shovels, no insurance, and no experience that lowballs your prospective customers, steals projects, and then leaves your customer high and dry after collecting a down payment. In HVAC, he's called "Stan-In-A-Van."

Dude-in-a-Van means well. Really, he does. And he may seem like a good deal with rates that are quite a bit less than an agency... and he can do it ALL! A good deal, right?

Not so fast.

Here are a few issues with hiring Dude-in-a-Van. For the purposes of explanation, let's call him Dave, which may or may not be the name of several "IT-professionals-turned-marketers" who have given ill-advised marketing guidance to several of my former clients... like the IT guy who turned OFF the phone number -- that was listed on their website, Google My Business, and dozens of prominent directories used by customers -- for one of our garden center clients. Good job, Dave.

Dave isn't readily available during business hours

Dave doesn't do this full-time. He works 9 to 5 at Kinkos and on his freelance projects after hours. Dave might have kids, another job on top of his day job, too many clients, a time-intensive remote control car hobby, and/or is otherwise not so great at communicating with you.

I can't tell you how many clients we've acquired at Ramblin Jackson who have been waiting for months to have simple edits made to their websites or for a password for a critical social media account that Dave set up. Even worse, Dave holds their domain name hostage by registering it under his personal account, and then goes rogue when it's time to let another vendor work on "his" website.

> Dave knows "enough to be dangerous" with SEO, Social Media, Graphic Design, Web Development, Google Adwords, Video, Facebook Ads, Psychology, etc.

Dave often knows "just enough to be dangerous" about critical things like website development, hosting, security, email, domain name setup, and SEO. If you ever have a vendor tell you he "knows enough to be dangerous" about anything pertaining to your sales, marketing, finances, or operations — run! Run and pray. Head for the hills!

A prime example of Dave's handiwork

Below is a screenshot of a Keyword Ranking report for a former client. (I always like to keep tracking

clients in our analytics software for a little while —
just to see what happens... and to tell them "I told
you so!")

The client didn't think we were doing any work
during our monthly maintenance plan (and
charging too much besides) because her rankings
were so strong and traffic was so consistently
great. She figured, "I'm all set, so there's no more
work to be done. Goodbye."

We parted ways amicably, and she went on to hire
Dave, the Dude-in-a-Van.

About four months after firing my agency, the
client called me and said, "What's happened? My
website has fallen off the first page of Google and
my phone has stopped ringing. Sales are down.
Whatever was working before isn't now. Can you
help?!"

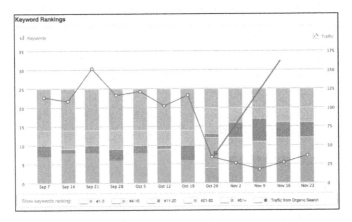

The zigzag line in the graph represents traffic to the client's website from organic search (the result of doing SEO). The sharp decline, where the arrow is pointing, shows when the number of people visiting the site plummeted, after she stopped using our services.

The bars in the graph represent five different levels of keyword ranking on Google. You can see how the client's rating fell drastically from the top of the first page, where we want to be, to pages 3-5 and even lower.

If that weren't bad enough, the **client's website was hacked and redirecting to porn**!

"Honey, I think there's something wrong with the computer."

Dave, who led the client to believe he was an expert at website development, hosting, and SEO, designed the site using an old WordPress theme that couldn't be completely updated because it was built without a framework. As such, it was vulnerable to attack and, for that reason, got hacked.

While Dave was able to remove some of the malware installed on the site, when he put it back up, he did not install *any* of the SEO settings. By then, the client was only ranking on the first page of Google for her business name and related names. That means that no one was finding the site (or her

business) using any relevant keywords. What a
disaster!

Luckily, we keep multiple off-site backups of client
work and were able to help the client *mostly*
recover.

How much did hiring Dave actually *cost* in this
instance? How much business did the client lose
during this down period that could have been
prevented? **$60,000.**

The company lost $60,000 in business during
their peak season while their website was
hacked and
redirecting to porn.

(Dave charged $3,000 less than me.
He gave them a good deal, right?)

I've learned the hard way that when it comes to
hiring people for a service, if you think you're
saving money, there's likely a large cost that you
won't realize until later.

I once hired an attorney who "knew enough to be
dangerous" about employment law. I used his
employee agreement template (admittedly without

even really reading it or taking the time to comprehend it), which he sent to me for free (without ever meeting with me to discuss my specific business needs).

I didn't fully understand what the agreement said but thought it was better than nothing and, since an attorney sent it to me, felt it must be pretty good.

Years later, there was an issue with an employee. The agreement I was using conflicted with my state's laws and put me in a much more compromising position than not having an agreement at all.

The same thing happened with a bad bookkeeper who almost put my company out of business.

Lesson learned the hard way,
multiple times:
When it comes to hiring people to do
critical tasks for your business,
find the best vendors possible.

Work One-on-One
with Me and My Team

If you've tried the DIY, employee, wrangle your own team of freelancers, or Dude-in-a-Van route and found that it took more time than you had to spare or didn't get you the results you needed to grow your business, you may be ready to hire a professional digital marketing agency.

Finding, hiring, training, and managing all the people to do all that's required is a lot of work — and an agency will have done that for you already.

Just like you'd want to talk to a real estate attorney about your real estate needs and an employment attorney about your employment needs, make sure that you talk with a digital marketing agency (one that *is an expert at marketing local businesses*) about your marketing needs.

Ramblin Jackson has over nine years of experience working with more than 300 local businesses throughout the country. **We love local!** In fact, it's all we do - and we turn down any business that isn't a good fit for what we do best. When you work with Ramblin Jackson, you'll have a dedicated account manager who helps you clarify your business goals, create a digital marketing strategy to achieve them, and work with you long-term to grow your business.

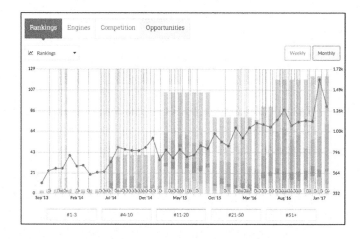

My favorite part of working with local businesses is helping them grow. Above is a screenshot of keyword ranking and traffic data for a client we've been managing for more than four years.

We've been doing everything that I've described in this book: building links, getting reviews, posting blog posts, managing social media, creating offers with email marketing, Facebook advertising, posting videos — and it's all paying off beautifully. There are 40 competing businesses like this one in the same city, but my client ranks consistently in the top three positions. Organic search -- people finding them through Google searches -- represents their number one source of new clients.

If you're wondering if digital marketing could help you increase your sales, contact us to learn how Ramblin Jackson can refine your business's digital marketing strategy.

There are lots of Dudes In Vans, freelancers, agencies, etc. Like I said in the Branding section -- what truly makes a business different is *their values* and the *way they do things.*

Core Values: Ramblin Jackson's Core Values

1. Be On-time and Prepared to Add Value

2. Craftsmanship in Life & Work, Especially on Fridays

3. Create Profit and Results with Integrity

4. Grow or Die

5. Be Human (& Pick Up the Damn Phone)

6. Be Professional

7. Raise the Stakes

If you want to work with a high-performing team that won't waste a minute of your time and help you grow your business, reach out to see how we can help.

We'll create a custom plan designed to optimize your website to drive more traffic and leads.

Take the Local Business Digital Marketing Quiz

> Wonder if digital marketing will work for you?
> Find out instantly with the Digital Marketing
> Quiz at ramblinjackson.com/quiz/

Take Action, Now

Regardless of whether you contact us for help, choose the DIY approach, or talk with your existing team, take action now. If you don't, you can be sure your competitors will.

Get started with a free consultation — your Marketing Strategy Meeting! Call us at (303) 544-2125 or visit our website, ramblinjackson.com/schedule/

Key Takeaways From Get Started With Digital Marketing

- Digital marketing requires a variety of skill sets to be done well.

- If you hire your employees to do your digital marketing, be sure to give them clear guidelines, expectations, and also sufficient time to do it during work hours.

- Beware The Dude-in-a-Van!

- Do something. Take action. Grow your business. Take the quiz: ramblinjackson.com/quiz/.

Bibliography

Introduction

[1]McDerment, Mike. Breaking the Time Barrier: How to Unlock Your True Earning Potential. Freshbooks, 2013

[2]Gerber, Michael. E-Myth Revisited: Why Most Small Businesses Don't Work and What to Do About It. Harper Collins, 1995

Chapter 1 - How Today's Consumers Find Local Businesses

[1]I-Want-To-Buy-It Moments: Mobile's Growing Role in a Shopper's Purchase Decision. Think with Google, 2016

[2]The Digital Consumer Study. Local Search Association, 2017

[3]Micro-Moments Now: Why you should be the adviser consumers are searching for. Think with Google, 2017

Chapter 3 - Lay the Foundation for Growth with Strong Branding

[1]Wickman, Gino. Traction: Get a Grip on Your Business. BenBella Books, 2012

Chapter 4 - Disqualify Bad Prospects with Professional Web Design

[1]State of Create. Adobe, 2016

[2]Bargas-Avila, Javier. Users love simple and familiar designs – Why websites need to make a great first impression. Google Research Blog, 2012

[3]Google Search Console. www.google.com/webmasters/tools/home

Chapter 5 - How to Get Found by Your Perfect Customers with Local SEO - Part 1

[1]LaFerny, David. A Complete Glossary of Essential SEO Jargon. Moz, 2007

[2]Google My Business. www.google.com/business/

[3]Moz 2017 Local Search Ranking Factors

[4]Improve your local ranking on Google. www.support.google.com/business/answer/7091?hl= en

[5]What does voice search mean for your local SEO strategy? Search Engine Watch, 2011

[6]How Mobile Search Connects Consumers to Store. Think with Google, 2016

[7]Google AdWords Keyword Planner. www.adwords.google.com/home/tools/keyword-planner/

[8]Moz Keyword Explorer. www.moz.com/mozpro/lander/keyword-research

Chapter 6 - How to Get Found by Your Perfect Customers with Local SEO - Part 2

[1]An update on doorway pages. Google Webmaster Central Blog, 2015

[2]Ellis, Miriam. Overcoming Your Fear of Local Landing Pages. Moz, 2016

[3]2017 Local Search Ranking Factors. Moz

[4]Moz Title Tag Preview Tool. www.moz.com/learn/seo/title-tag

[5]Moz Open Site Explorer. www.moz.com/researchtools/ose/

Chapter 7 - Are You the Best? Become THE Choice with Strong Reviews

[1]Improve your local ranking on Google. www.support.google.com/business/answer/7091?hl=en

[2]Google Trends. www.trends.google.com/trends/

[3]Local Consumer Review Survey. BrightLocal, 2016

[4]Ibid

[5]Showcase your site's reviews in Search. Google Webmaster Central Blog, 2016

[6]Rating schema. Schema.org/Rating

[7]Northwestern Study Volume 1: From Reviews to Revenue. Power Reviews

[8]Zetlin, Minda. Here Are the Best Ways to React to Criticism, According to 13 Experienced Speakers. Inc.com, 2017

Chapter 8 - Drive Repeat Business with Email Marketing

[1]LSA 16. Local Search Association, 2016

[2]Yodle Survey: Consumers Want Local Businesses to Improve Websites, Reward Loyalty and Increase Communication. Yodle, 2015

[3]2016 State of Marketing. Salesforce, 2016

[4] Science of Email 2014, Hubspot

Chapter 9 - Leverage Social Media Marketing to Engage and Convert

[1]Vaynerchuk, Gary. Crush It!: Why NOW Is the Time to Cash In on Your Passion. Harper Studio, 2013

[2]Shepard, Cyrus. 10 Illustrations of How Fresh Content May Influence Google Rankings. Moz, 2016

[3]Kennedy, Dan & Kim Walsh-Phillips. No B.S. Guide to Direct Response Social Media Marketing: The Ultimate No Holds Barred Guide to Producing Measurable, Monetizable Results with Social Media Marketing. Entrepreneur Press, 2015

Chapter 11 - Measure Results

[1]Marchant, Ross. Phone Calls & Search Ranking are Most Important Local Search KPIs. Brightlocal, 2018

[2]Moz 2017 Local Search Ranking Factors

Chapter 12 - Make the Sale

[1]Small Business Owners Don't Answer 62% Of Phone Calls. 411 Locals, 2016

[2]Oldroyd, James B., Kristina McElheran, David Elkington. The Short Life of Online Sales Leads. Harvard Business Review, 2011

[3]Kurlan, Dave. Baseline Selling: How to Become a Sales Superstar by Using What You Already Know About the Game of Baseball. AuthorHouse, 2005

[4]Kurlan, Dave. What Does It Mean for a Salesperson to Have SOB Quality? YouTube, 2014

**Chapter 13 - Beyond Digital Marketing:
Be Excellent. Be Local.**

[1]Luca, Michael. Reviews, Reputation, and Revenue: The Case of Yelp.com. Harvard Business Review, 2016

INDEX

B

books

80/20 Sales And Marketing, 287
Baseline Selling, 298
Breaking The Time Barrier, xx
E-Myth Revisited, xx
No B.S. Guide To Social Media Marketing, 246
Traction, 20

branding, 13

C

CMS. *See* website development

coaches

Blumenthal, Mike, 158
Herring, Wayne, 24
Kennedy, Don, 39
Killeen, Al, xx

Kreinbrink, Jim, 162
Kurlan, Dave, 297
Magner, Jeffrey, xxvii
Ramblin Jackson, 39
Swenk, Jason, 24

D

demographics
millennials, 4
senior women, 111

digital marketing, 315
automation, 246
foundation of, 10
landing pages, 246

E

email marketing, 183, 270
best practices, 190
calls to action, 197
click-thru, 198
direct response offer, 188
email newsletters, 189
frequency, 205
grow your list, 203
list segmentation, 197, 209
mobile, 194
new customer welcome campaign, 200
open rates, 198
selecting your software, 210
subject lines, 192
The CAN-SPAM Act, 208
video in email, 198

when to send, 206

F

Facebook. *See* social media marketing

I

interviews. *See* Ramblin Jackson, interviews

L

local businesses
   arborists, 83
   auto services, 118
   brick-and-mortar, 5
   dentists, 19, 59, 122, 311
      cosmetic dentists, 75
   doctors, 59, 122
   home repair, 19, 25, 29, 41
      window replacement, 23
   HVAC, 19, 324
   landscaping, 25, 29, 59, 63, 324
   lawyers, 19, 59, 122
   locksmiths, 19
   Pilates studios, 19, 110
   real estate agents, 19
   restaurants, 5, 59, 90, 217, 302
   service area businesses, 122, 294
   service businesses, 59
   therapists, 19
   yoga studios, 19, 29, 123

M

management

performance indicators, 274
recruiting, 255
    Facebook ads, 244
sales process, 282

measurement, 289

Excel, 287
How did you hear of us?, 279
impact on revenue, 281
point of sale, 283
QuickBooks Online, 283
SEO
    rank tracking, 278

mobile, 55, 65

mobile search, 3, 72
mobile search options, 88
nomophobia, 7

O

online reviews, 302

best wings near me, 157
GetFiveStars, 179
how to get reviews, 175
negative reviews, 169
reviews from the web, 36, 155, 156, 160
trust in, 159
where to get online reviews, 165
words used in reviews, 162
Yelp, 77, 177

P

photography, 59, 217, 218

professional photos, 80

R

Ramblin Jackson
    beef jerky club, 21, 299
    core values, 20
    interviews, 41, 63, 83, 254

recruiting, 27, 244, 255-6

S

sales, xx, xxi, 200, 289, 293, 297
    CRM, 282
    direct response offer, 245, 306
    disqualify bad prospects, 43
    niche market, 112
    perfect client, 98
    pricing, 48
    purchase decisions, 158
    repeat business, 183
    sales conversion, 296
    sales process, 293, 297
    trust, 251
    unique selling propositions, 28

search engine optimization (SEO)
    behavioral signals, 79
    citations
        NAP inconsistencies, 94, 98
    citiations, 91, 92
    geographic keywords, 136
    Google
        adwords, 71

local map, 71
my business, 72, 79, 156, 163
pay per click (PPC), 71
snack-pack, 71
keyword, 69
keyword research, 98, 102, 136
link building, 306, 308
links, 79, 146
local directories, 149
local landing pages, 125
local SEO, 67
mobile, 156
Moz, 67
NAP, 92
on-page SEO, 115, 126
internal links, 138
meta description, 131
optimized footer, 139
title tags, 128
URL, 132
rank tracking, 278
ranking, 69
ranking factors, 77
apps, 78
distance, 87
domain authority, 147
internal links, 228
local directories, 78
NAP, 78
page authority, 148
PageRank, 147
prominence, 87
relevance, 86

reviews, 78
site freshness, 227
schema, 120, 141, 168
JSON-LD, 144
search engine results pages (SERPS), 69
search query, 69
best, 90
customer journey, 5
glueten free, 90
near me, 90
open now, 90
SEO copywriting, 134
SEO keyword research, 134
website headers, 134

SEO. *See* search engine optimization

social media marketing, 215
blog, 229
FAQ, 229
Facebook
Facebook advertising, 235, 240
custom audiences, 239
data centric, 237
direct response campaigns, 245
lead generation, 244
Facebook election scandal, 235
Facebook Live, 268
General Data Protection Regulation (GDPR), 236
geographic hashtags, 224
hashtags, 224
Instagram, 224
social media post ideas, 217
Twitter, 224

stories

Beware the Dude-in-a-Van, 323

Free Cake, 204

How a Home Repair Contractor Tripled His Leads, 41

How One Company Got 10 Jobs within the First Hour of One Email Campaign, 187

How One Landscaper Uses His Website to Stand Out from Chuck-In-A-Truck Competitors, 63

How One Webpage Created Over $200,000 for a Pilates Studio, 110

How to Become a Big Fish in a Small Pond, 107

How Tony P Lost 30% in Revenue from NAP Inconsistencies, 94

My Famous Chicken Wings Experiment, 162

My Milkman Story, xxii

The Arborist Who Increased Sales 30% with Local SEO, 83

The Dentist Who Gives out Roses, 312

The Refrigerator Delivery That Wasn't Very Cool, 36

T

tips, 24, 60, 61, 102, 106, 135, 179, 198, 204, 224, 226, 229, 230, 239, 241, 295, 306, 308

V

video, 250, 268, 270

branding, 264

DIY smartphone, 259

non-profit fundraising, 266

recruiting, 255

testimonials, 252

where to host, 256

W

website development
 calls to action, 54, 137
 content management system (CMS), 46
 security, 58
 site speed, 47
 website headers, 52, 134
 website hosting, 57
 WordPress, 61

writing
 blog
  after the sale, 232
 copywriting, 24, 230

GRATITUDE

This book is dedicated first and foremost to my incredible wife, Kara, and our two boys Whalen and Wyatt. There's no way I could have possibly made it this far in business if Kara didn't help me stop dressing like a lumberjack (at least for meetings), make me get a proper men's haircut when I had a gross two-foot split-end ponytail, and continue to tell me to keep going even when the going gets tough. At a time when most women heard "unemployed" when I told them I owned my own business -- and I can't blame them for thinking that because I was a long-haired cigarette-puffing cheese-curd-eating flannel-clad mandolin-wielding PBR wildebeest -- Kara somehow saw potential. Thank you for believing in me, deer. Let's sell a bunch of these books and buy a camper like we've always wanted.

To Ralph E., the Good Boy, my #1 D.O.G., the "Moose", for helping co-found Ramblin Jackson and for being a good dog for a long time. See you on the other side.

To my parents, Bob and Patti, for teaching me to love the English language. Even hearing the pair of you bicker sounds like poetry. Thank you for teaching me to read, for teaching me to work hard every day, for attending every performance possible, for giving me the opportunities to be creative and experiment that you didn't have, and for leaving the newspaper out at breakfast with copy editing errors circled in red pen. You are nerds through and through and I love you.

To my talented circus freak sister, Kira Jostes O'Connell, for being the best big sister in the world and for being so supportive of all my creative pursuits. To my big brother, Brett, for making me tough and teaching me how to wrestle, swear, and use fireworks.

To Ramblin Jackson's COO Leah Leaves, for holding down the fort while I took the time to write this book and for your years of support of helping establish the company.

To Chris Woodley, for forever making me cringe when I see people taking videos in portrait mode on their smartphones, for putting in years of hard work as co-owner of Ramblin Jackson in the early years, and for teaching me nearly everything I know about making great videos.

To my coaches: Jason Swenk for telling me to keep going when I was close to closing; to Al Killeen for helping me kill nice-guy-itis and become a business warrior; to Hugh Liddle for teaching me to become a sales professional; and to Wayne Herring for coaching me to become a CEO and better overall dude.

To my talented book production team: Paul Chaney for copy editing; to Lezly Harrison for book formatting and production assistance; to Kyle May for creating the Foundation of Digital Marketing graphic and related book marketing items; to Oma for proofreading; and to Liv McCoy for designing the book cover and related graphics.

To my clients for trusting me with your hard-earned dollars to practice my craft and Create Profit and Results With Integrity for your business.

To the SEO & marketing folks from whom I continue to learn so much, especially: Rand Fishkin, Mike Blumenthal, Jeffrey Magner, Jim Kreinbrink, Perry Marshall, Dan Kennedy, Sarah Bird, Britney Muller, Miriam Ellis, Cyrus Shepard, Drew Dinkelacker, and all the school teachers who encouraged me and challenged me especially Mrs. Carbone, Mrs. Perez, Mr. Levinson, Mrs. Toast, Phil Koehl, Benjamin Percy, Dr. John Pauly, Phylis Ravel and the Marquette Theatre department.

To you! Thank you for reading my book. Post a photo of this book in a neat location on Instagram and tag @jackjostes and I'll send you beef jerky or high quality almonds as a gift. For real. Do it.

ABOUT THE AUTHOR

Jack Jostes is the President + CEO of Ramblin Jackson, a digital marketing agency based in Boulder, CO that has helped over 300 brick-and-mortar and service area businesses grow their sales with local SEO, website design, and digital marketing since 2009. In addition to creating a weekly video series, *Friday's Ramblin Roundup*, Jack loves public speaking and regularly presents at national and local business conferences. Jack was named one of *BizWest's Boulder Valley 40 Under Forty* in 2017, and Ramblin Jackson was a 2018 Finalist in the *Colorado Companies to Watch*. He enjoys living in Colorado with his wife and two boys, playing bluegrass mandolin, brewing kombucha, fly fishing, practicing yoga, and working.

To book Jack Jostes as your keynote speaker, podcast guest, or marketing strategist, call (303) 544-2125 or email booking@ramblinjackson.com. ramblinjackson.com/speaking/

Made in the USA
Middletown, DE
27 January 2020

83639761R00215